SEASIDE ENTERTAINMENT IN SUSSEX

A wartime show bill with the name of the town removed for security reasons

W H Johnson

S.B. Publications

By the same author
Early Victorian Alfriston
Crime and Disorder in Late Georgian Alfriston
Previous Offences
Alfriston Past and Present
The Kent Murder Casebook
The Macaroni Dancers and Other Stories
Sussex Disasters
The Surrey Murder Casebook
Kent Stories of the Supernatural

First published in 2001 by S. B. Publications,
19 Grove Road, Seaford, East Sussex BN25 1TP

ISBN 1 85770 222 0

Designed and typeset by CGB, Lewes
Printed by Tansleys The Printers
19 Broad Street, Seaford, East Sussex BN25 1LS
Tel: 01323 891019

CONTENTS

ACKNOWLEDGMENTS

The author wishes to express his gratitude and indebtedness to Edward Thomas, author of *The Playhouse on the Park,* and Max Tyler, Historian of the British Music Hall Society, for their generous assistance with the draft of this book. Whatever flaws remain are entirely the author's responsibility. Sincere thanks are also owed to Pauline Hubert of the Sussex Music Hall Society and Sue Watts both of whom provided the author with useful information.

PICTURE CREDITS

Many people have taken time to hunt out photographs and illustrative material. Thanks for this go to the British Music Hall Society and the library and museum staffs at Bexhill, Brighton, Eastbourne, Hastings, Bognor Regis, Littlehampton and Worthing. The staffs of Leisure Parks Ltd and Eastbourne Borough Council's Tourism and Community Services Department have also been most helpful. Particular mention should be made of the contributions of Barbara Bone, Rebecca Fardells, Julian Porter, Norma Seal, Kathy Wellings and Dr Sally White. The author is deeply grateful to Christopher Horlock who has kindly allowed use of items from his personal collection of photographs.

INTRODUCTION

The purpose of this book is to provide a broad survey of entertainment on the Sussex coast from the end of the eighteenth century to about 1970. These were the great years of seaside pleasures and performances which were richly diverse and immensely satisfying. It is not simply an exercise in nostalgia that makes us look back to those days. In recalling them we are bringing to mind a vibrant past and a brilliant tradition.

The demand for entertainment sprang up alongside the growth of the resorts. First came the privileged classes with their demands and their expectations. They wanted to be entertained as they were in London. Then followed the masses, conveyed by train to spend their Sundays by the sea and later granted annual holidays to stay longer, for a week or a fortnight even.

While Brighton and Hastings had little hesitation in providing a wealth of varied entertainment for this new expanding clientele, Bexhill, Eastbourne and Worthing initially greeted them with less enthusiasm. But such large crowds, with money to spend, could not be ignored. Eventually the whole coast from Bognor and Littlehampton to Hastings laid on entertainment on their seafronts, on their piers, in their Winter Gardens, Theatre Royals and Hippodromes.

It is of that now vanished period of entertainment with which this book deals – the days when every Sussex resort had for its residents and its visitors a show to go to. Inevitably I have omitted mention of many performers who ought to have merited inclusion but I am working on a small stage and I cannot people it as fully as I might have wished. After all, the potential cast is enormous. Nevertheless, I hope that the reader will find some entertainment here.

W H Johnson
Eastbourne
February 2001

A handbill of William Cooke's Equestrian Circus which, by royal command, gave a display of acrobatic horsemanship at the Royal Pavilion, Brighton, on 18 September 1830.

1

CURTAIN UP

The leisured classes 'discovered' the Sussex seaside in the middle of the eighteenth century. Encouraged by Dr Richard Russell's *Dissertation on the Use and Value of Sea Water* they came in ever-increasing numbers to its small coastal towns and fishing villages for the good of their health. They demanded lodgings of an appropriate standard and expected to be offered entertainment equal to that provided for them in London and at the new spas of Bath and Buxton. After all, there was more to life than being dipped in the sea, even if it was good for the health. And if one had to drink a daily pint of sea water – not that Russell went so far as to advocate such a remedy though others of his profession did so – at least there ought to be some associated pleasures and compensations.

The sea water craze, which began in the mid-eighteenth century and lasted well into the nineteenth was a vital factor in the development of the Sussex seaside. The 'dipping' was simple enough. All a gentleman – or a lady for that matter – had to do was to climb the steps to the rear door of a bathing machine which was simply a horse-drawn hut on cart wheels. Once inside he took off his outdoor clothing, slipped into a voluminous costume, and opened the door at the front. Here, at the foot of another flight of steps, was the dipper who would grip him by the shoulders and dip him several times in the water. No question of swimming.

The Prince of Wales's favourite dipper was 'Smoaker' Miles, who always referred to his client as 'Mr Prince' but the best known of all the dippers was Martha Gunn, who died in 1815 at the age of eighty-eight. Fifty years later, the Great Vance, one of the most celebrated of music

'Now for an all over, Mrs Plash', is the caption to this engraving on the pictorial writing paper favoured by eighteenth century holidaymakers.

hall turns, was successfully singing *Come to your Martha,* a comic song about the still affectionately-remembered Brighton character. Its chorus goes:

'Come to your Martha, come, come, come,
The water is hot in the sun, sun , sun.
Don't shiver dear, there's nought to fear
But come to your Martha, come.'

By then there were 250 bathing machines drawn up on the segregated beach, on their sides the names of their owners – GEORGE MAY (late J WRIGHT) Gentlemen's Bathing and R PEARCE, Ladies Bathing.

It was the arrival of members of the aristocracy, and above all of the royal family, which gave that extra push to the popularising of Brighthelmstone, where there had been a season of a sort from the 1750s.

Henry, Duke of Cumberland had made regular annual visits between 1779 and 1784 and was sufficiently entranced to recommend it to his nephews. So down came the two future kings, George, Prince of Wales and his brother, William, Duke of Clarence. And with them came their entourages of sycophantic and irresponsible courtiers with their own trains of equally aimless hangers-on. Feckless and spendthrift though they were, their presence was enough to promote Brighton as a place in which to live for part of the year and, as a consequence, as a centre of entertainment.

Among the great figures of fashion were Mrs Fitzherbert, who married Wales, who in the end betrayed her; and one of the most brilliant comic actresses of the age, the delightful Dora Jordan, who lived with Clarence for twenty years and bore him eleven children before he so cruelly dismissed her shortly before coming to the throne as William IV.

Worthing, too, had its royal connection with the arrival there of the Princess Amelia, George III's youngest daughter, hoping that sea air and sea water would cure her consumption. She felt, too, that it would be near enough for her brothers to visit her and far enough away for her not to be too frequently embarrassed by their sometimes outrageous behaviour. The Duke of Kent, father of Victoria, had his home at St Leonards and the Princess Charlotte favoured Bognor, later referred to by Victoria as 'dear little Bognor'. Untainted by rowdy royals, it retained that respectable quality so prized by many and so despaired of by others who sought something rather more saucy, more earthy and more raucous.

It was the royals and the aristocracy who determined the new shape of the seaside towns, the kinds of buildings that would be the envy of the world. In the Steine at Brighton, the Prince of Wales had his great Pavilion built on the site of the farmhouse where he was living. And others of that wealthy community who had settled there, and in the other villages and towns they had recently colonised, would eventually come to occupy great sweeping terraces and elegant squares.

For their leisure, and they had much of that, they had their Assembly Rooms for concerts, lectures, dancing, banquets, cards, billiards. Libraries were built for them, with all the latest books from London, the latest novels of Walter Scott, the most recent poetry of Mr Coleridge and Mr Wordsworth. They had their theatres, too, for they were sophisticated and knowledgeable.

In the early years of the nineteenth century Brighton had its Theatre Royal; Hastings its short lived New Theatre in Bourne Street; Worthing its Theatre Royal in Ann Street and as the years wore on Bognor, too,

The Theatre Royal in Ann Street, Worthing.
Photo: Worthing Museum and Art Gallery.

and Bexhill and St Leonards would all be catering for the increasing demands for entertainment. Brighton soon had half a dozen theatres; Hastings, by 1900, two; Eastbourne, three.

The twentieth century lost some of the stock of fine, old theatres but would add some of its own, notably the modest looking White Rock Pavilion at Hastings; the controversial De La Warr Theatre in Bexhill which to Spike Milligan's regret escaped German bombs in wartime and the Congress Theatre at Eastbourne, opened in 1963 and so plainly solid and ill at ease in its surroundings in a conservation area which includes the Winter Garden and the Devonshire Park Theatre.

It was the development of the railway service in the 1840s that brought new kinds of visitors from London to the Sussex seaside. There had long been a regular and frequent stage coach service from the capital to Brighton but this could not carry crowds of people so cheaply and so quickly as the trains. The day out and the cheap weekend excursions brought many thousands to the coastal towns where previously the coaches had brought a few hundred. Middle class England, or rather middle class London came to Brighton, Hastings, Eastbourne, Worthing and other places increasingly served by rail. In their wake came working class England, its members' demands for entertainment equally as strong as those who had preceded them.

In the early years of the nineteenth century, Brighton had the Royal Circus at the bottom of Carlton Hill. It was a popular pleasure garden which, as its name suggests, housed a circus in addition to other facilities. Sadly this enterprise failed as did Ireland's Pleasure Gardens with its Gothic buildings which for three years in the 1820s offered a wide range of attractions including a maze, a grotto, frequent fireworks displays and cricket matches. Perhaps their failure was attributable to the variety of other diversions then available in the town.

The Swiss Gardens at Shoreham, built in 1838, remained popular with all classes for fifty years. They attracted huge crowds at weekends when excursions by train from Brighton and Portsmouth became possible. The visitors could stroll round the ornamental lake with its tiny passenger steamer and wander through the very well-kept gardens. There were balloon ascents and firework displays, as well as bowling greens and archery for those so minded.

For many years the Swiss Gardens were a fashionable place to meet. There visitors could take tea in the large refreshment room, see the plays put on in the theatre, dance in the elegant ballroom, or perhaps have a game of Chinese billiards or bagatelle. Only the arrival of increasing numbers of badly behaved and disorderly pleasure seekers led to the decline in its popularity. It was the prospect of such

This rustic observatory was a popular feature of the Swiss Gardens at Shoreham.

disorderly conduct that for so long persuaded the citizens of Eastbourne and Bexhill to resist any Sunday entertainment although in the end they were forced to yield.

Elsewhere, the great tragedians and comedians of the legitimate stage would come to thrill. The sublime Sarah Bernhardt, false leg or no, was as popular in Brighton as in the rest of Europe. And there were circuses, too. Some were fixed within the theatres; others toured, coming in great wagon trains like an invading army to camp within the towns for a few days before moving on to new venues.

The world of music had its municipal orchestras with their guest stars of international renown playing in Winter Gardens and Kursaals, in the White Rock Pavilion, the De la Warr and the Dome. There was fine music in the bandstands, too, and on the piers – another of the Victorians' contributions to architecture and entertainment. And, for a time after the Second World War, even the most respectable towns would offer drag artistes, all-in wrestling and nude shows.

As for popular entertainment and popular music – they were located in the music halls and their successors, the variety theatres. If Sussex contributed little to music hall – though there are saucy music hall songs and jokes enough about Brighton – its variety theatres have been of some significance. And most important in giving pleasure to people were the concert parties, the great end-of-the-pier shows such as Clarkson Rose's *Twinkle*, Sandy Powell's *Star Wagon* and the celebrated *Fol de Rols* whose performers were the cream of their profession.

So, let's go on with those shows . . .

2

ALONG THE PROM, PROM, PROM. . .

The fashionable who had first come to the seaside in the search for seawater cures increasingly abandoned the seafronts where, with the advent of the railways, the majority of the entertainers paraded themselves. The beach and the seafront had been invaded and taken over by tradesmen and the working classes and hordes of performers had followed in their wake.

At Bexhill the threat of low entertainers was largely averted by Earl de la Warr, who obliged the council of which he was mayor – and a Socialist one at that – to pass bylaws which made public performances on the seafront illegal. There were a few fortune-tellers and occasional sand artists but nowhere near as many as at some other seaside towns.

Eastbourne council had passed a series of effective bylaws to keep undesirable performers away from public places. It was a successful resort, its population swelling from 6,000 in 1860 to 43,000 by the turn of the century and it aimed to attract a genteel clientele. Its only notable busker in the 1900s was a Scottish piper who appeared each summer in full regalia. He was ultimately enlisted by members of the Presbyterian church to train their Fife and Drum Band and thus he passed from the state of being a street entertainer to becoming a respectable musician.

Less popular resorts could never support the sheer numbers of entertainers – amateur, semi-professional and full-time professional, ranging from the brilliant to the unspeakably awful – who thronged the seafronts of Brighton and Hastings.

At Bognor, in the early twentieth century, Frank Bale had a regular pitch in front of the Royal Hotel. In his clown's costume he was accompanied by a talking cockatoo, a monkey and a dog. He also sang, accompanying himself on either banjo or guitar. Often he called on the children to join in his act as he juggled and clowned away the days. His rewards were possibly quite small but he gave immense pleasure to thousands in a less sophisticated age.

Fred Bale with his dog Towzer.

Who else then performed for the hordes of trippers at the principal resorts? What kinds of acts were on show for the working men and women, the clerks and shopworkers, the farm labourers and dockers, on their days out? It is clear that over the years there was little radical change and what the visitor encountered in the 1880s was not very different from what he might see in the 1930s. And what he saw in Brighton, on the beach and on the promenade, was very little different from what he would see at Bognor – granted its Regis from a recuperating King George V in 1929 – and other resorts along the Sussex coast.

At each, or all, he might see sand artists working on the beach with combs and knives, sticks and brushes, forming out of the damp sand pictures of castles and cathedrals, images of kings and warriors – competent works which would disappear with the next high tide.

At Hastings, the artist was one-armed. By the side of his sculpture would lie a handwritten card which read:

'To earn a living on the sand
I do my best with my one hand.
If you will throw a copper small
I will thank you, one and all.'

14

Sand artist Ted Child with an example of his work.

At Worthing the sand artist's lines were:

> The tide is coming in, my labour to destroy.
> If you will drop a copper now
> You will fill my heart with joy.

Ted Child, whose family held the concession for the fruit stalls along the promenade at Eastbourne, was a sand artist and his favourite pitch was just west of the pier from where admirers of his work threw down pennies. Local councils were responsible for the beach above the tideline and they required anyone involved in a commercial venture on the strand to apply for a licence which might, or might not, be granted. In Hastings in 1938 a man was fined for sand-scratching without a licence, just as was another who had tried to amuse the public with a wind-up gramophone and a couple of mice. For the most part, the regular buskers and entertainers were licensed, but undoubtedly there were many occasionals who just turned up on a fine Sunday in the hope of making a few shillings.

15

Opportunism and entertainment go hand in hand. If a performer does not try to find himself a public, he will never prosper. Nevertheless, at Hove the police could see little of merit in the activities of the Happyjackers, barefoot urchins on the lower promenade, whose sole contribution to the pleasure of others was to call out to strollers to throw pennies down to them for which they would scramble and fight.

Accordionist 'Blind Harry' had a pitch on Brighton seafront.

There was plenty of music. There were German bands and regular military bands and hurdy-gurdy men with their monkeys, blind accordionists and one-armed fiddlers, harpists, one-man bands and players on the spoons, harmonium players, unaccompanied singers and Ethiopian serenaders. Add to these the stilt-walkers, the wrestlers, the street acrobats, the men who juggled barrels with their feet, the fire-eaters and the conjurors, the escapologists and chapeauologists who, by a turn or two of the brim of their felt hats, became the Emperor Napoleon or a highwayman or a lady of the streets or a country bumpkin. There were ventriloquists and performing dogs. There were even dogs that told fortunes – dogs clever enough, according to their masters, to tell your future from the cards. Italian women at Hastings trained birds in cages to perform similar tricks.

The adults had been the first to be entranced by the psychopathic Mr Punch and the marionettes such as the 'enchanted Turk' whose limbs flew apart and assumed new and independent characters or whose bodies turned into balloons. Like their professional rivals, the Punch and Judy men, marionetteers were to be popular for the next 150 years. On Hastings pier, at the beginning of the century, was Madam Haydee and her Marionettes. Later, there was Professor Day whose puppets appeared as Chinese jugglers, drunken stilt walkers, acrobats, dancers and boxers. In 1939 his stepson, John Alston, took over the act, presenting shows from 10.30am until 9pm, when the last performance of the day, lit by oxy-acetylene lamps, had a live pianist accompanying a concert party of puppets.

The Punch and Judy men have not entirely gone away. They still perform in a few of the resorts. Some are still remembered with affection, which is remarkable really when the content of the act is considered. Even though the central character is a wife-beater, a child murderer, and a killer of policemen, the Punch and Judy show is loved on the sea fronts.

Tom Kemp, who kept a live crocodile in his bath as part of his act, performed on Brighton's West Pier for many years in the 1920s and 1930s. His routine with the sausages was said to be unsurpassed. On Worthing pier in the 1950s Gordon Hamilton gave eighteen ten-minute Punch and Judy shows every day. And Percy Press – 'Uncle Percy' to countless children for thirty years from 1951 at White Rock – was probably the best known of all the Punch and Judy men. All of these voices called out over the decades, urging the visitors to join in the fun, to listen to the music, to give the 'bottler' a copper or two, to come onto the West Pier to see Professor Doughty and his Performing Dogs or Professor Powsey diving off the same pier while mounted on a bicycle. Or why not at Hastings watch G W Houghton, billed as the Human Torpedo, performing 'one of the most difficult feats ever attempted'? Houghton would offer a

Professor Powsey cycling into the sea from Brighton's West Pier.

challenge to the world. He would wager £25 that he would propel his body a full 33 yards 15 inches in the sea with his head totally immersed. Or why not, between the wars, respond to Biddy Stonham, the Hastings tubman? His encouragement, especially to young ladies, to join him in his seaborne tub regularly worked and Biddy, his black top hat decked with flowers, would sit his uncertain passenger in the tub and then would balance on the rim, twisting round the tub until it overturned and all parties fell into the water.

Certainly there was enough free outdoor entertainment for the many thousands who thronged the promenades.

3

OH DOO DAH DAY

In the time of the day excursions, before holidays with pay became an established fact, among the great seaside attractions for the trippers were the blacked-up minstrels. They were everywhere – as solo buskers and duos or in troupes of half a dozen or so performing in the open air. They presented their shows in 'fit-ups' – flimsy canvas awnings which offered them some slight protection against the wind and rain – or they might make arrangements with the local council for the use of a hall in seriously bad weather and many councils, aware of their pulling power, were only too willing to accommodate them.

Dr White Eye ran a minstrel group at Littlehampton. During the 1914–18 war a troupe composed of soldiers from Summerdown Convalescent Camp performed on the middle deck of Eastbourne pier. For many years the Original Hastings and St Leonards Minstrel Troupe hired a seafront pitch, close to the landing stage of the pleasure yachts, *Skylark* and *Albertine*. There were half a dozen or so in the party, their songs backed by a harmonium. In addition some members played ukeleles and bones. As with all minstrel troupes, their strength lay in their singing. They were expected to sing so-called 'plantation songs' so that their repertoire inevitably included *Swanee River, Golden Slippers* and *Camptown Races*. Sentimental home-grown ballads and lively comic songs were also included. The latter, however, contained none of the broad humour of contemporary music hall songs.

Between musical items, some members of the troupe were expected to provide comic relief, the butt of their humour being the rather pompous Mr Interlocutor, the compere and straight man. Entertainment provided by the minstrel troupes was all good, clean, wholesome fun 'fit

Dr White Eye's minstrel troupe at Littlehampton.

for all the family' as their posters would say. Their pitch was often marked off by the 'nigger ring', a low board a couple of feet high. Inside this, where seating was sometimes provided, the audience paid. But those outside were able to see and hear for nothing. For this reason, the minstrels, like their successors the pierrots, employed one of the cast as a 'bottler' to circulate among the audience collecting coppers in a bottle. The use of a bottle for the collection rather than a plate or a cloth cap was traditional – and practical. Those collecting had not always been honest and by sleight of hand had sometimes managed to purloin some of the take but try slipping the odd coin out of a bottle.

Capturing audiences was essential in such a highly competitive enterprise. Usually one of the troupe was designated 'Uncle' and he was responsible for getting the attention of the children and making them identify with him. He would lead them in singing and would encourage them to come on stage to recite or to dance or play a trick on Mr Interlocutor. Such strategies frequently ensured that the children concerned paid a second or third visit.

There were also popular black or blacked-up turns on the stage. In the 1870s the *Era Almanack* listed 145 'Negro Delineators' performing in English theatres and music halls. Brown, Newland and Le Clerq were regulars at the Brighton Alhambra with their famous comic sketch, *Black Justice.* Appearing there at other times were Sam Redfern, billed as 'black comedian' and Lily Harold, Coon Vocalist and Dancer. In 1891, at the Eastbourne's Theatre Royal, later renamed the Hippodrome, Mr Charles Harrington's Company presented *The Octoroon*, the first play to attempt to describe faithfully the condition of blacks in the southern states of America. The programme promised that:

> 'In the Course of the Piece A TROUPE OF REAL NEGROES will introduce Songs, Glees, Choruses and Dances, representing Plantation Life in their Native Home.'

It was, however, the great touring minstrel parties who were mostly responsible for the popularity of minstrel music in the last half of the nineteenth century. The three most famous groups were the Christy Minstrels, the Mohawks and the Moore and Burgess troupe. The Mohawks, who were based at Islington, played four-week seasons on Brighton's West Pier each year from 1898 to 1903. They also played month-long seasons at Hastings Pier where

The Mohawk Minstrels published their own topical songs. *The Wonderful Octopus* was a favourite at Brighton Aquarium.
Photo: C Horlock.

21

the charge for entry to the pier was twopence plus an additional penny for entrance to the performance.

The Mohawks usually numbered about forty. Traditionally they wore blue coats with red and white buttons, white shirts with large collars and huge bow ties. Their trousers had red and white stripes. As the curtain rose they appeared sitting in a semi-circle, the orchestra on tiered seats above them. Some members of the troupe played banjos, concertinas and cornets. Between songs there was banter between the seemingly serious compere, Mr Interlocutor, who sat in the centre, and Mr Bones or one of the other minstrel comics, who played either the tambourines or knacker bones and who always sat at the extreme ends of the semi-circle. Ballads and comic songs usually took up the first half of the Mohawk programme but these versatile and accomplished singers might devote the second half to Scottish, Welsh or Irish songs. On other occasions they might offer concerts of sacred or operatic music.

In 1900, prior to their amalgamation with the Mohawks, the Moore and Burgess troupe from St James's Hall in Piccadilly went on a farewell tour

Eugene Stratton.

of England. They said their goodbyes to St Leonards in a show on the pier in June of that year and on the same tour they appeared at Eastbourne. This troupe had in earlier years appeared at the Royal Concert Hall in St Leonards and at Worthing's Theatre Royal. Among the cast on at least one occasion was the American, Eugene Stratton, billed as 'The Dandy Coloured Coon', a comedian, singer and dancer known principally for three songs, *Lily of Laguna, Little Dolly Daydream* and *I May be Crazy but I Love You.*

For all that Stratton was famed for these songs and was later extraordinarily popular on the variety stage using the same material, it is said that he was not an especially good singer. As Rex Harrison was to discover, when playing

22

the part of Professor Higgins in *My Fair Lady*, for some performers speaking the words is just as effective as singing them and this is how Eugene Stratton performed his songs. His dancing, especially his soft shoe shuffle, was said to be as light as thistle down. He appeared to be drifting across the stage. Dan Leno, Little Tich, G H Elliott and the 'White Eyed Kaffir' G H Chirgwin, all of them favourites of the variety stage, had also 'worked black'.

By the turn of the century the minstrels had been ousted in popularity by the pierrots. Sometimes the two types of entertainer existed side by side on the same seafront but the minstrels became fewer and fewer. Yet the minstrel tradition never quite died. In the 1920s and 1930s a popular radio programme, *The Kentucky Minstrels*, ran for several years. In 1950, Hastings tried with some success to revive the 'old time beach nigger minstrels' in a new 850-seat foreshore enclosure adjoining the Marine boating lake. The crowds were delighted by the antics of Tambo and the Dark Town Glee Club in a two hour performance but the show was not retained for long. And then, of course, there was the Black and White Minstrels Show which kept millions glued to their television sets on Sunday evenings in the Sixties and delighted theatregoers when it went on the road.

A postage stamp size stage and a few parasols and Harry Joseph's pierrots are in business and, below, a deckchair audience for a show by the troupe at Littlehampton in August 1908.

4

BLACK POM POMS AND POINTED HATS

The professional outdoor performers who so enlivened the seafronts of our resorts worked in all weathers, putting on three or four performances a day. As long as there was an audience, no matter how wet, cold and gusty the beach, the show went on and the bottlers, smiling on the outside, persuaded damp, shivering audiences to pop a coin in the bottle. It was not an easy profession to belong to. By present standards the stage fittings were primitive. There was no stage lighting, no microphones, no sound effects and the artistes played against raging winds, in incessant drizzle, sometimes to miserably thin audiences. When, as at Hastings in 1919, a marquee blew down in the night during a gale and the seats and benches were scattered to the four corners, the performers had to re-erect the marquee and find the seating before the next day's performance could take place. An even worse fate had befallen a concert party at Seaford in 1914. After the marquee was destroyed in a storm, the show was abandoned and the cast thrown out of work.

Over the years the minstrels, in their modest 'fit-ups', had faced these hazards of seaside entertainment. So did those who came to take some of their audiences from them. It is difficult to account for the quite remarkable ousting of the minstrels in favour of the pierrots. Quite suddenly, in the early 1890s, a new style of performance arrived and almost at once the well-loved minstrels, after fifty years of unabated popularity, were on the slide.

Impresario Clifford Essex, on a visit to France, had been much taken with the make-up and costumes of a charming mime play which had featured a pierrot. How compelling he thought the costume; how rather

25

more dashing than his own small group of accomplished concert singers in their customary evening dress. He even liked their name. On his return, he fitted out The Marguerites in French pierrot costumes. When in 1891 they played before the Prince of Wales and his friends at Cowes Regatta their future seemed assured. Essex changed their name to the Royal Pierrots.

Soon pierrot groups were springing up throughout the country. Every beach had its pierrots with their loose white silk blouses and pantaloons, their conical hats topping the black silk bandanas round their heads. The blouses and hats carried the big, black trademark pom-poms. Some groups wore a white face make-up, not unlike that of clowns, but unsurprisingly, in view of its being an unpleasant mix of zinc and lard, not all did so. The pierrot rage, which lasted at full pitch until the 1914 war, was under way.

At times in some resorts, in addition to the inevitable buskers, there might be three or four concert parties. These could be minstrels or pierrots or perhaps, after the first enthusiasm for the pierrots had waned, there might be a party which played the first half in pierrot costume and the second half in evening dress or in blazers, white trousers and yachting caps. Whether minstrels, pierrots or concert parties, they were usually excellent singers, providing a wide range of songs, comic, operatic, sentimental and rousing. Ye Merrie Minstrels, for example, who appeared at several Sussex resorts at this time comprised a bass and a baritone, a contralto and a soprano, a pianist and a comedienne-chanteuse. Every effort was made to appeal to the genteel and respectable. In 1915 Clarkson Rose was temporarily dismissed from Edgar Allan Brown's company in Eastbourne for singing *Who Bashed Bill Kaiser?* The patriotic sense of the song was not in dispute but the lyrics were adjudged 'too music-hally.'

In the early years of the twentieth century, on Hove Lawns, previously forbidden to performers who had been restricted to the beach, were the White Coons – pierrots sure enough, but their title carrying an echo of the black-faced troupes. At Littlehampton there were three parties, run respectively by Frank Spencer, Harry Joseph and Edgar Allan Brown. Their audiences sat in the open on deck chairs or on wooden benches. At St Leonards, Clifford Essex's Pierrots performed on the pier.

Uncle George and his Thespians and the banjoist Walter Howard's

Jollity Boys, in addition to companies belonging to Fred White and Will Pepper, appeared simultaneously at Bognor. Obviously there were quite enough summer visitors to go round. Uncle George's company was on the beach at Bognor for many years. The men dressed in boaters, green blazers and white ducks and the females in bright chiffon. They did the familiar pierrot programmes of songs, dances and brief sketches. The performances lasted until the tide threatened to wash away George's portable harmonium, the piano, the collapsible stage and the canvas backcloth. Noel Coward cherished the memory of how, as a child, he won a box of chocolates in a talent contest on Uncle George's stage and he immortalised the troupe in one of the scenes of *Cavalcade*.

When Uncle George's troupe finally disbanded, and his pitch was taken over by Uncle Duggie and his Merrymakers, old George returned each year to Bognor to trundle his harmonium around the streets, along the seafront and in and out of the pubs.

Wallis Arthur, credited with being 'one of the most refined comedians on the English stage,' was also one of the most successful of pierrot and concert party impresarios. He had companies appearing in Bognor, Hastings, Eastbourne and in other English resorts for forty years.

He was all too well aware of the need for decent seating and for comfortable permanent buildings for his artists to perform in. It is thanks to people like him and Johnny Hunter, the director of entertainments at Hastings in the early 1900s, that such buildings as the White Rock Pavilion came into being.

Wallis Arthur's company had

Seaside Personalities

"The Stage"
31st MAY 1934
CLARKSON ROSE LOG BOOK.

But a link with Uncle George, and in fact a link with all that is Bognor's great al-fresco past, is still here in Uncle Duggie Campbell—who with his Merrymakers provides ideal open-air entertainment where children can take their parents. In spite of rather cool weather and an early Whitsun, a large crowd were watching this capital show the other afternoon, and Duggie Campbell's indefatigable work throughout the show was something of an education for many performers—especially the beginners in our business. This seasoned Adeler and Sutton trouper knows all the tricks, and his infinite resource was a delight to watch. No wonder he is a great favourite in Bognor, where his cheery and kindly personality has endeared him to everybody.

"Uncle Duggie"
Of Bognor

Jack Sheppard's Brighton Entertainers with, behind the pianist, young Harry Sargent who was to find fame as Max Miller, Brighton's Cheekie Chappie.

begun in a temporary structure near the lifeboat pavilion at Hastings. Later it played in marquees or bandstands or on the piers at Eastbourne, St Leonards and Hastings, generally giving two performances a day. If there was a strong onshore breeze or a sea fog the troupe at Hastings sometimes moved from the beach to Alexandra Park or to the Central Cricket Ground. Arthur's principal comedian for seventeen years at Hastings was George Blackmore and his other leading comics were Franklyn Vernon on Eastbourne pier and Fred Rome at the Olympian Gardens in Bognor. In all of the resorts where Arthur's parties performed, the notices outside his pitches hinted that the best people were likely to be in attendance. They read: 'Wallis Arthur's Season Nightly at Eight O'Clock' and then, after giving the full cast list, 'Carriages at 10.15pm'. He had an acute awareness of what his audiences wanted in the different resorts and made every effort to give it to them.

At Brighton the most successful troupes were run by Jack Sheppard whose pre-1914 pierrots, The Highwaymen, underwent a post-war change of name to become Jack Sheppard's Brighton Entertainers. The pierrot craze had waned and instead of a floppy white outfit with black pom poms and pointed hats the men wore white trousers, boaters and striped ties and the women smart dresses with cloche hats. Usually numbering seven or eight, they performed on a small stage with a piano and with a chair for each artist. One of their pitches was opposite the Metropole Hotel and another opposite Madeira Walk. Sometimes they appeared on the West Pier either on the open deck or inside the Pavilion. One of Jack Sheppard's cast, hired in 1919, was a local boy, Harry Sargent, who was to become Max Miller.

Bexhill, always careful of its reputation, was blessed with several good pierrot groups and concert parties. The Olympia Quartet, which first appeared in 1900 on the beach near the Metropole Hotel, established a loyal following who went with them when they appeared at Egerton Park. Other entertainers appearing in the park, or in the Shelter Hall, included the Adeler Combination, the Red Rovers and Cardow's Cadets.

Madam Whitworth Rose and Charles Resti's Concert Party performed in the bandstand on West Parade and in 1909 Will Tissington and Harry Collard's Poppies played at the newly opened Pergola in fine weather and, when it rained, in the Shelter Hall. In 1911, when the council invited Farley Sinkins' Quaviators to the Pergola, Tissington and Collard formed the Coronets and were given a licence to use 'certain premises near the coastguards cottages for public singing, dancing and music' on all days except Sundays. They were told, when making their licence application, that 'in Bexhill many people like to be quiet on Sunday and Sunday entertainment might not meet with their wishes.'

At Worthing a troupe called the Worthing Whimsies appeared on the pier in the early 1900s and the Yellow Dominoes played opposite the Steyne as did another concert party whose name no one can recall but whose material was said to have been 'rather coarse'.

On the pier at Eastbourne Felgate King and Elsie Mayfair produced *Pier Revels* every summer from 1915 to 1934. King was a musician who had enjoyed a successful West End career and his wife was a fine mezzo-soprano. Their later productions had a style and polish far removed from the best efforts of six-handed fit-ups on windswept beaches. It was the style of entertainment that their better paid, better dressed, and better fed audiences wanted and shows like *Twinkle* and the *Fol-de-Rols* were waiting in the wings to provide it.

The bandstand on the De La Warr Parade, Bexhill, where Herr Wurm's White Viennese Band played in the summer months. *Photo: Bexhill Museum.*

The carriage drive along Bexhill's seafront and the Kursaal theatre and concert hall.

5

ON THE BANDSTANDS AND THE PIERS

The Sussex seaside resorts had, by 1900, either bandstands or band enclosures on their promenades or their piers. They were regarded as a physical indication of a town's solidity and worth and there was, at the time, a great following for brass music. Many resorts had their own brass bands – perhaps the fire brigade band or police band – but Brighton, a garrison town, could also rely on military bands from such regiments as the Household Cavalry and the Royal Artillery.

In the bandstand on the Baths Promenade at Hastings the jaunty little Austrian, Herr Wurm, a plumed shako on his head, led his Blue Viennese Orchestra. At Bexhill his orchestra wore white uniforms and played much the same mixture of classical and popular music. In yet another of his incarnations in the 1890s, the ubiquitous Wurm conducted another of his Viennese orchestras on Brighton's West Pier and bandstand. Among his musicians at one point was Gustav Holst, a student of trombone at the Royal College of Music, eking out his scholarship funds.

For many years prior to the First World War, Dr John Abram, who had founded the Hastings Conservatoire, organised regular concerts on the pier and by 1900 Hastings had a summer band which gave concerts in Alexandra Park, the Archery Gardens and in St Leonards Gardens. This orchestra, along with guest military bands, gathered crowds of up to 4,000 for their outdoor programmes at weekends.

At Worthing, where the Lido now stands, was a 'birdcage' bandstand on which the Borough Band, resplendent in elegant uniforms, would play. After the pier was built in 1860 a nine-man orchestra was put under contract to play on it for three hours a day 'weather and circumstances

Elegant Edwardians promenade past the bandstand at Worthing

permitting' and later on the German Rhine Band presented programmes there daily. In 1889, when it seemed that there would always be enough people more than willing to pay to listen to music, a pavilion was erected at the far end of the pier.

Prior to the First World War among those playing at Worthing was Mme Florence Sidney and her twelve string Ladies Orchestra and Adam Seebold's Chamonix Orchestra which had earlier performed as the Swiss Band and the Jungfrau Kapelle. On the seafront bandstand at Bognor, you might perhaps have come across Tipper's Band or the Blue Hungarians, said to have been formed by the Austrian or German members of an abandoned and penniless circus band who had adopted Bognor as their home. Or what about the ladies' ten-piece orchestra about which the enthusiastic reporter of the *Bognor Observer* was moved to write:

'O, listen to the band! please do. I am referring to the Blue Zouave Ladies Orchestra. Their season is young yet, but I say without hesitation that it is the best Orchestra I have heard at the pier for years. Comparisons are odious, but give me a ladies' orchestra. Here you do not have to look at a double-bass player with an Ally Sloper nose of a ruddy hue, or a bleary eyed flautist, but the eye as well as the ear is charmed by the curved lip of a fair (it may be brunette) musician using her sweet breath to produce melodious notes from the flute, while cornet blowing can only serve to round the soft curves of a lady's face.'

Many of the Victorian pleasure piers with their long wooden decks projecting out to sea are adorned by oriental-type domes, Empire-style concert halls and great flourishes and curlicues of ironwork. They are florid, fanciful, exuberant and, for the most part, the best of them reflected the remarkable Pavilion at Brighton, which announced to the world that great public buildings need not be too serious, too stuffy, but rather that they ought to be at times cheerful and if the occasion called for it, a trifle vulgar. After all, if a fantasy palace built for a prince's pleasure could demonstrate some of this jolly swagger, then why not a pier which was dedicated to the people's pleasure?

At first they were designed for promenaders, with some wrought iron seats, a windbreak down the centre, and a landing stage at the seaward end. Later they had their own band stands, theatres and concert halls, their peepshows and their funfairs, their bowling alleys and their penny-in-the slot machines and became a major feature of the seaside entertainments scene.

Let us look at them, pier by pier, beginning with:

Bognor

Mary Wheatland was Victorian Bognor's answer to Brighton's 'Queen of the Dippers' Martha Gunn. Mary worked on the seafront for some sixty years, teaching swimming and looking after the bathing huts. Even late in life she would dive off the pier, clad in her long serge bathing dress, and then stand on her head in the water, waving her buttoned booted feet in the air. She boasted, when she retired, that none of her bathers had ever drowned.

The Bouquets, originally run by Wilby Lunn and later by his daughter Betty, usually had a company of about fourteen, including four dancers and two pianists, in the Pier Theatre. They were all expected to sing, dance and take part in sketches and to perform a solo lasting about eight minutes. The programme usually changed five times a week during the summer season, placing considerable pressure upon the performers.

Brighton: The West Pier

The concert hall, built in 1894, could seat audiences of up to 1,000 and it was later transformed into an even larger theatre seating 1,500. Top of the bill turns appeared here, often on Sundays – their rest days from the Theatre Royal or the Empire. Among them would be George Robey, Harry Tate, Florrie Forde, Nervo and Knox, the Mohawk Minstrels, Max Miller and Albert Whelan.

The West Pier was considered more select than its easterly neighbour and was popular with visitors to the grand hotels who were not put off by the sideshows, possibly because they were less suggestive than those on the Palace Pier. After all, performing fleas were not vulgar. How could they be when they taught seriously minded and respectable people about the wonders of Nature. Furthermore, fleas possessed the work ethic. They could be seen diligently drawing water or driving a hansom cab. They turned windmills or fired cannon. Some fought duels with steel swords and others, reflecting the world beyond, would take a drive in a carriage drawn by other fleas.

Brighton: The Palace Pier

The Palace Pier's somewhat ripe reputation was established in its earliest days. There were always novelties to draw the crowds, always freak shows, shooting galleries, waxworks, circus acts. Its mutoscopes which

The original Marine Palace which gave the Palace pier its name was practically a Royal Pavilion look-alike. It was remodelled in 1910. *Photo: C Horlock.*

at the turn of a handle flipped over pictures to provide the illusion of movement, were considered at the time to be most daring although today *Her Saturday Night,* showing a young woman preparing to take a bath, and *All Alone* would not raise the temperature. But *What The Butler Saw* or *The Parisian Can-Can* was hot stuff for Victorian and Edwardian Brighton. *I'll Say She Can* and *The Naked Truth* might be all right for the Palace Pier but certainly not for its more select neighbour to the west.

Nelson Lee's wooden, clockwork-driven models, showed gruesome haunted houses and churchyards. A prisoner during the French revolution was followed from the condemned cell to the point where he lost his head at the guillotine. In the 1930s, Lee's working model of the execution of Mary, Queen of Scots, drew huge crowds.

Eastbourne

The theatre on the pier had seating on two levels for an audience of up to 1,000 and presented shows all through the year, although until 1906 there was no heating. It had a bar, offices and a cafe and, although many day trippers brought their own food with them, others ventured into the tea room where in 1905 they could buy a roll and butter or a cup of tea or coffee with biscuits for twopence. A pot of tea cost fourpence and for another twopence they could buy a slice of Genoa cake or a boiled egg or a ham or tongue sandwich or an ice cream. Lemonade, ginger beer, lime juice or milk was twopence a glass.

The new theatre complex had a camera obscura in its windowless dome which revolved on huge ballbearings turned by a hand windlass. As the roof turned a silver surfaced mirror and lenses mounted at an angle of 45 degrees picked up the image of the scene outside, projecting it onto a white emulsioned bowl about six feet across. In pre-cinema days, or at least, during the film industry's infancy, the camera obscura was a huge novelty for those who paid to see it.

Hastings

The Joy Wheel was a great attraction on Hastings pier. It was housed at the shore end in a circular building which had seats for spectators round the interior. In the centre of the floor was the wheel on which all the participants sat. According to newspaper reports it 'revolves at a giddy

Hastings Pier. The Joy Wheel was in the big circular building on the left.

speed and hurls its victim yards along the glazed floor'. Fortunately the walls were cushioned.

Among the fortune tellers on the pier were Professor Cullen and Madame Lena, 'The World Famed Scientific Palmist, Psychic Adviser and Clairvoyant' who claimed a kind of superiority in being not a fortune teller but a 'Fortune Guider'. She promised 'no guess work.'

St Leonards-on-Sea

This pier, which was demolished in the 1950s, had a magnificent pavilion at the shore end which, until the First World War, was known as the Kursaal and was the first home of the municipal orchestra under its conductor, Julian Clifford. The interior was lavishly appointed and could seat 750. There were also anterooms for ladies and gentlemen as well as smoking and reading rooms. There were no slot machines but in 1910 a men's beauty contest was held which, it was said, 'occasioned much hilarity'. A dance hall and refreshment rooms were added and a roller skating rink.

By 1930, the once elegant structure was severely run down and it was bought cheaply by the Lannon brothers whose improvements – a zoo at the sea end, all-in wrestling and a man with a loud hailer in a motor boat making announcements – were all too vulgar for some residents. Perhaps in the old days nothing quite as tasteless as the funeral of Bonzo would have been so widely proclaimed in the local press. Good publicity certainly – good for the pier and for the brothers' investment but for the more staid it must have smacked of a decline in standards. For after all, who was Bonzo? A performing flea who in the middle of his act had been struck by a bolt of summer lightning – or so they say, for there is no record of any other damage.

On a Sunday evening Professor E Bradley Warren had been playing to a crowded house when fate struck. The manager of the motor race track on the pier organised a subscription so that the Professor might purchase a replacement for Bonzo and a special coffin. A day or so later, with Jack Dale's band playing Chopin's *Marche Funebre,* a cortege processed solemnly along the pier. Proprietors of all the sideshows, who had contributed wreaths, attended as well as visitors. The last post was sounded, a bell tolled, there was a two minutes silence, a volley was fired and Bonzo's mortal remains were cast into the deep.

Worthing

It was a wet and stormy Easter Monday in 1913 and only thirty people turned up to listen to the McWhirter Quintet's programme of light music. Part of the way through the programme they were forced to flee for their lives for the pier was being blown apart by near hurricane force winds. The whole centre structure was washed away and the South Pavilion left stranded out at sea. It was quickly rebuilt and re-opened and by the mid 1920s had acquired a new pavilion at the landward end with a stage and seating for 900. The colour scheme of blue and gold, the trellised walls and the big hand-painted lamp shades of Venetian design were highly attractive and audiences flocked to see the concert parties of the period, including the quaintly-named Glad Pilots Concert Party and the Mischief Concert Party supported, of course, by the Ladies Orchestra.

Disaster struck again in 1933. A blaze that could be seen as far away as Selsey Bill destroyed the South Pavilion and much of the decking had to be stripped away to prevent the fire spreading to the landward end.

Madame Florence Sidney's twelve piece Royal Navy Ladies Orchestra on the pier at Worthing.
Photo: Worthing Museum and Art Gallery

Two years later, at a cost of £18,000, the pier's South Pavilion was re-built and included a solarium on the ground floor and a wide first floor balcony for sun worshippers. Happily it was business as usual at the landward pavilion where the *Moonlight Follies* and later the *Fol-de-Rols* and *Twinkle* played to packed houses. A post-war facelift and the addition of the Denton Lounge made this multi-purpose building the resort's major entertainment venue. Concerts of classical music, revues, social functions, dances, all-in wrestling, musicals, top of the bill variety acts . . . they were all at the Pier Pavilion.

6

WHEN THE CIRCUS COMES TO TOWN

Whatever the glamour of the theatre, whatever the pull of the music hall and the generally innocent appeal of the pantomime, could any of these match the unique qualities of the circus? Was there in any theatre or hall, no matter how glittering its furnishings, regardless of how well known its stars, quite the attraction of the circus? Consider until recent years the sheer discomfort of most circus marquees – the hard wooden benches, the lack of heating, the primitive sanitation – and compare this to the relatively luxurious interiors of the pier pavilions, the Theatres Royal, the Winter Gardens.

Yet the arrival of a circus raised the heart-beat for no other form of entertainment could, in so short a space of time, demonstrate so great a degree of skill, quite so much shimmering novelty, as did the riders, animal tamers, acrobats and wire walkers as they went through their spangled acts. And possibly because we recalled the acts rather than the names of those who performed them, they came to us fresh each time yet always with a hint of the exotic as though they were from a different realm from the rest of mankind.

They did not always travel. The circus did not always come to town. Not infrequently it was a permanent feature which only in the middle months of the year went on tour. In London from the late eighteenth century Philip Astley's circus was a great draw. Here, huge casts of up to 150 performed dramatic pieces on horseback. Dick Turpin rode to York in Astley's circus and Richard III died while horses plunged around the riderless king at the Battle of Bosworth. This was acrobatic riding at full gallop. Astley's fixed circus set the standard for the rest of the country and for all time. Cooke's short-lived Royal Circus in Brighton in the early nineteenth century was, like all the early circuses, mainly comprised of equestrian acts. There were few other animals but there were tumblers and clowns on the programme. The highlight of one show was 'James Cooke who, on horseback, threw off costume after costume to show himself as sailor, Dutchman, African, Harlequin, Columbine and others'.

The Ginnett family's circus in Brighton was renowned throughout the country. The founder, Jean Pierre Ginnett, had left France and sought his fortune in England with a modest busking act of four canaries and a monkey. He later had enough money to buy a pony which told fortunes, pointing a forefoot at cards which held the secret of love, life and happiness. This then enabled him to buy a modest tent. At the time of his death he left £80,000, a stud of 300 horses, a large tented travelling show and permanent circuses at Brighton, Torquay and Belfast.

The Brighton circus, the Hippodrome, was principally the brainchild of Jean Pierre Ginnett's son, Fred. It was built in Park Crescent and opened in 1876. Designed on the Paris Grand Cirque pattern, its ring was fifty feet in diameter and the building could accommodate up to 3,000 spectators. A smaller hall which Ginnett built behind the Hippodrome was named the 'new Grand Olympia.' Here he staged such spectaculars as *The Battle of Ulundi* with real Zulus and '(by permission) real soldiers.'

John Frederick Ginnett's tomb in Woodvale cemetery, Brighton. *Photo: C Horlock.*

Many of Ginnett's major competitors were, by now, staging vast representations of Waterloo, the Afghan War, the Sudan campaign, the relief of Ladysmith and the Zulu Wars. In Sanger's *Relief of Khartoum* there were real rifles and real field guns firing blanks. In one

The horses get their heads down as Ginnett's circus takes a break at Lewes on its way to the next booking.
Photo: C Horlock.

spectacular Sanger employed 700 men, 100 camels, 200 horses, the fifers and drummers of the Grenadier Guards and the pipers of the Scots Guards.

On Christmas Eve, 1888, Ginnett's Hippodrome and Olympia opened with a show which included a hundred horses, elephants, bulls, deer and scores of other animals and fifty artistes, including clowns, jugglers, wire walkers, acrobats – every possible kind of traditional circus act. But within two years its days as a circus had ended and it was transformed into the Gaiety Theatre. Ginnett turned his attention to his palatial 5,000 seater New Hippodrome and Circus which opened in 1891 in North Road, near the railway station, but he died the following year and his family, who continued the circus tradition, sold the New Hippodrome. It became the Eden Theatre.

Circuses are, perhaps, best known for touring. In 1845 Edwin Hughes' circus paraded through Hastings with a 'Burmese Imperial state carriage and throne' drawn, so the proprietor proclaimed, by 'royal male and female elephants'. Hughes announced that he was: 'determined to make every effort for the Amusement of the Public and

Crowds watch a circus parade through the streets of Littlehampton.
Photo: Littlehampton Museum.

begged most respectfully to inform them that the Royal Male and Female Elephants will bathe in front of the Marine Parade at six o'clock in the evening'.

In 1898 Barnum and Bailey's 'greatest show on earth,' after visiting Eastbourne, moved on to Hastings by train. So enthusiastic was the public that some camped out in the streets overnight for the next day's grand parade from West St Leonards railway station to Hickman's field in St Helens. Heading the parade were forty bay horses drawing the band carriage which, like all the conveyances, was brightly painted in blue and red and gold. Next came several open cars, each pulled by four white horses, and each containing caged animals – tigers, lions, leopards, panthers, pumas, hyenas, bears and wolves. Inside each carriage sat an animal trainer. These were followed by the female trick riders in 'natty costumes' and Roman chariots, with charioteers appropriately costumed, and a chariot carrying musicians. Another group of eight wild beast cars was followed by 'Asiatic riders' mounted on camels and behind them, elephants with howdahs. Then came more extravagantly coloured cars, including the coaches of Cinderella, Little Red Riding Hood and Mother Goose. Somehow, in this world of caged violence and fairy tale, it does not seem altogether out of place to know that 'the Bluebeard chariot, showing the fabled monster in the act of slaughtering one of his wives who had discovered his secret,' was drawn by six pretty zebras. A troupe of Japanese performers in a dragon car came next and then the throne of King Ferdinand and Queen Isabella of Spain with mounted outriders, grandees and nobles. The steam whistles of a calliope brought up the rear. Had not St Andrew's arches prevented the passage of some of the vehicles the procession would have been even longer.

At the turn of the century came the spectacular Wild West shows which purported to show how life really was on the great prairies. In August 1903, Buffalo Bill Cody's Wild West Show came to the Old Toll Gate Fields in Eastbourne. His cast included the so-called Congress of Rough Riders of the World. Racing across the open spaces of the Wild West, located temporarily on the Sussex coast, were Mexican cowboys, warlike Sioux and the cavalry of many nations. There were demonstrations of lassooing, cracking the whip and bronco busting. The US Artillery fired huge cannon and a prairie wagon was attacked by Indians 'of the type familiarised by the illustrations which grace the covers of the penny blood and thunder publications'. Enclosed by vast canvas walls, the show played to vast audiences. Cody, an obscure army scout, had been brought to public notice through the cheap and highly exaggerated dime novels of Ned Buntline. Thereafter, he enacted a spurious fiction through his circus but true or not, Cody's Rough Riders thrilled thousands.

What is so remarkable about the old circuses is their scale. The Great Allied Show of Alexandra, Howe and Cushing's circuses which came to the coast in 1908 described itself as 'the Largest and most Talented Olympic Equestrian Combination ever gathered together'. There were a hundred performers and 120 ponies and horses as well as a host of other animals. In the huge marquee which could accommodate 10,000 there were two rings as well as a central stage so that five acts could appear at the same time. And the midday parades brought Eastbourne and Hastings to a standstill.

Lord George Sanger's famed circus always arrived in an enormous procession. Seventy wagons trundled through towns carrying tents, seating, property, tableaux, backstage equipment. There were boxing booths to be transported and all manner of rides such as the Sea on Land Ride in which patrons sat in mock yachts. There were chairoplanes,

helter skelters, big wheels and in later years, dodg'em cars. The band, seated in an open wagon, played songs of the day while a dozen elephants and as many camels and up to 150 ring horses and ponies were led by their trainers, and in their cages, tigers snarled and lions roared. And calling out to the populace were ringmasters, clowns, acrobats, contortionists and jugglers.

Alexandra's Great Circus, which was still claiming to be the largest travelling circus in the country, returned to Eastbourne, Newhaven and Seaford in June 1921. Among the attractions were the: 'THE FAMOUS TEN REAL WEZZAN ARABS, the greatest bounding marvels of the age, the most amazing and foremost exponents of Exotic Athletics'. The announcement boasted that 'This Troupe is engaged at the enormous salary of £100 weekly.'

George Wombwell, whose freak and animal shows regularly

Presentation programme printed on satin for the mayor of Hastings in 1825.

accompanied the Sanger circus around the country in the 1850s, felt no qualms about advertising a fight between a lion and a pack of mastiffs. It was an immediate sell-out at a guinea a seat. Sadly for those who had paid to see the contest, the ancient lion refused to fight and his replacement, being younger, saw off the dogs. This may give some idea of how attitudes have changed over the years. If cruelty declined, the interest in animal performers continued. The popular Royal Italian Circus, which appeared at several Sussex venues, was at the Royal Concert Hall in Hastings in 1908. There were dogs, a baboon, a zebra, a bear, several goats and monkeys and 'all take part in the fancy dress balls, the suppers and the many other wonderful tricks gone through'.

In the 1940s the Royal Imperial Circus performed at the Eastbourne Hippodrome and in the 1950s the 'fresh and vital' Circus Rosaire played the same venue on several occasions. To White Rock for two weeks in 1951, came *Circus Revusical*, a combination of musical comedy and circus. Audiences were treated to Coady's lions, Fossett's bulls and ponies, bears, trapeze monkeys, clowns, jugglers, comedians and Clem Merk, allegedly 'the only trainer to enter the lion's cage unarmed.'

Tom Arnold's Ice Show at Brighton turned into an Ice Circus in some years with performers from big tops all over Europe. Billy Smart's great show regularly fitted Hastings, Worthing, Brighton and Eastbourne into its itinerary and Fossett's Mammoth Jungle Circus, with a marquee accommodating 3,000, appeared on the Downs at Bexhill and on the Seaside Recreation Ground at Glyne Gap.

The Victorians were interested in the aberrations of nature and in the 1880s they had no difficulty in putting sideshows on display in the entrance hall of the Brighton Aquarium. Thus a gawping public could stare at Krao the Missing Link, snigger at Mme Alphonsene on the Globe, point at the Tiger Lady, and jeer at the Bear Boy. The side shows which accompanied circuses always had freak shows, most of them displaying animals born with some marked genetic eccentricity. Five-footed goats and two-headed sheep were common. But most popular were the men and women who perhaps might otherwise have suffered a worse fate than public display if left to make their own way in a cruel world.

George Wombwell's menagerie included the Heaviest Man on Earth, The World's Ugliest Woman and Beautiful Marie, the Giant Schoolgirl. In the many side shows attached to Buffalo Bill's circus when it came to the county was 'a number of freaks, both of the natural and artificial persuasion', the greatest attraction being 'the smallest midget in the world', a 21 inch tall, twenty two year old woman. Another of the exhibits was the Human Ostrich who was said to consume 'repeated doses of indigestible articles'. The freaks who travelled with Barnum and Bailey's circus on its 1898 visit included a giantess and a dwarf, a double jointed man and a human skeleton. And then there were the fraudulent objects such as Lord John Sanger's Madame Stevens, the Pig Faced Lady who, bonneted, mittened and garbed in a frock and shawl, sat in a chair and appeared to answer questions. In reality, Madame Stevens was a bear with a shaven face. When she was questioned, a boy concealed below the seat into which she was strapped, prodded her, causing her to grunt. Without doubt, the animal spent most of its days heavily drugged.

The variety theatre as well as the circus regularly took what advantage it could to put the bizarre before its audience. What was odd, eccentric, strange could always be found some place on the programme. As late as 1948 a show at Eastbourne Hippodrome entitled *Would You Believe It?* included Elroy the Armless Wonder who opened beer bottles with a corkscrew and extinguished candles with a pellet gun. On the same bill was the so-called Human Wax Doll and Lofty Evans who, at the age of twenty two, was said to be more than 9ft tall and, said the programme: 'They maintain that by the time he reaches the ripe age of thirty he will attain 10ft'.

'Little people' Melitta and Willy were always billed as 'potpourri entertainers'.

At other times on stage there was Jack Joyce, the one legged dancer, and the Hylton Sisters who were Siamese twins, as were the violin-playing Blazeks. These were billed as remarkable speciality acts, but nothing that these performers did would have been remarkable had they not had some kind of disability. That they had to some degree overcome their disability is undeniable but the impression remains that they were regarded by theatre managements as no more than freaks.

Some may feel that other groups of people were being exploited in similar fashion. Dwarfs and midgets, for example, were always a popular element in circus and stage shows. In the 1880s among the best known was Mr Charles Pearson, the Sussex Dwarf. On Eastbourne Pier in 1913 twenty five 'Wonderful Midgets' presented a miniature circus in which twelve midget ponies were introduced, and a number of clever equestrian feats performed. There was tight-rope walking, wrestling, humorous interludes, singing and dancing, and a selection by their own brass band. In 1952 Burton Lester's Midgets included Harry Behrens, said to be 'the smallest man alive at 2ft 6ins'. He came on stage in a carriage pulled by a cat.

Even if today midgets are still employed in theatres and circuses, one hopes that they are less crassly regarded. Fortunately, the old-fashioned freak shows, which were so often of the grossest kind, have disappeared from our stages. Today few circuses have animal acts. Most Sussex seaside resorts have banned them as being cruel, degrading and humiliating to the animals.

The Theatre Royal in New Road, Brighton – built in 1806 and still going strong.

7

I WANTS TO MAKE YOUR FLESH CREEP

In no theatre, it has been said, did melodrama flourish as it did at the Theatre Royal in Brighton. The plays were based for the most part on simple tales and their central characters portrayed as ordinary people. The acting was far from the realistic style of today's stage, the actors gesturing in great sweeps, their voices indicating their emotions. The language was always fanciful and inflated. No matter where the hero was born, even if he was the poorest of the poor, he spoke more than correctly, mouthing high-sounding opinions and long-winded intentions regardless of the urgency of the situation. So too did the deepest-dyed villains. Only the humblest characters were allowed to use everyday language.

The exaggerated acting, not unlike that in some of the earliest silent films, was accompanied by 'expressive' music. For example, in the stage directions for one speech in *The Blind Boy*, a much performed piece, is:

'Music - expressive of his agitation';
'Music – his eyes filled with tears. He wipes them';
'Music – walks about in great agitation, with hasty strides';
'Music – walks about as before'.

In other plays the orchestra was required to play 'music of doubt and terror' or 'threatening music.'

The setting was usually in some hostile environment. The climaxes, in particular, placed the heroes and heroines in apparently insurmountable dangers which they always nevertheless escaped. *The Miller and his Men* ended with a violent explosion. At the end of *The Innkeeper's Daughter*, which played Hastings in 1827, the last scene had Richard escaping but he is, according to the play bill, 'wrecked upon a Rock.'

'Mary seeing his danger, puts to sea in a LARGE BOAT, mans and works the sails alone, reaches the rock, and SAVES HER LOVER!!!'

When it was presented at the Eastbourne Hippodrome in 1901, Act 3 of *Denounced* was described in the programme in equally compelling terms:

'Destruction of the bridge – suspended in mid-air! Leap for life! Friends in need! Not dead yet! Faithful to the end!'

And who could possibly resist the offerings at Brighton's Gaiety Theatre in Park Crescent Place in the 1890s for the sheer verve and technical know-how which allowed such elaborate effects and which must have thrilled audiences? Even the Gaiety's regular rowdy gallery patrons must have been silenced sometimes. Maybe they held their collective breath when trains thundered past each other, or perhaps when a boiler exploded on a Mississippi steamer. Surely they held hands to mouths in astonishment when, in that lurid melodrama *The Slums of London*, the hero, tied to a stake, struggled free just in time to throw the dynamite into the river before it exploded.

Not that the critics always admired such populist offerings. One wrote of the often-performed *Lights of London*:

'If anything it is too real, too painful, too smeared with the dirt and degradation of London life, where drunkenness, debauchery and depravity are shown in all their naked hideousness. Amidst buying and selling, the hoarse roars of costermongers, the jingle of the piano-organ, the screams of the dissolute, fathers teach their children to cheat and lie, drabs swarm in and out of the public house, and the hunted Harold, with his devoted wife, awaits the inevitable capture in an upper garret of a house which is surrounded by the police'.

But the mass of theatre-goers loved their blood and thunder until, towards the end of the nineteenth century, even they saw through the unlikely plots and the ham acting. At the Gaiety the gallery frequently heckled the actors. In *Lucky Star* as one lay dying, there were shouts of 'Read the burial service' and 'Bring on the stretcher'. It was difficult to sustain credibility in the face of such regular derision and in 1900 the Gaiety closed and the Grand, which had always had a fine reputation for its melodramatic productions, turned its back on such popular trash – or seemed to do so until after the First World War, when melodrama had a sudden resurgence.

Actor-manager Andrew Melville, centre, in a tense scene from *Robespierre or the Reign of Terror*. *Photo: C Horlock.*

In the 1920s, Andrew Melville, the actor-manager of the Grand, made his theatre the home of sensational melodramas, some of which he wrote himself and others which were written by his brothers Walter and Frederick. Now the Grand's programmes included *Maria Marten or The Murder in the Red Barn*; *The Face at the Window*; *The Crimes of Burke and Hare*; *Dracula*; and *Jack the Ripper* which the Lord Chamberlain allowed to be staged only after certain cuts to the script were made. The blood-curdling *Sweeney Todd* had Melville in the central role. He delighted huge audiences with his performance and whenever the demon barber despatched another victim, the enthusiastic regulars up in the gods echoed his bloodthirsty threat, 'I'll polish him off!'

The crowds flocked to see Melville's *Robespierre*, described as 'The Most Daring Play that has yet been attempted'. And the posters declared:

'NO CHILD UNDER 14 ADMITTED UNLESS ACCOMPANIED BY AN ADULT'

It included a scene in which beautiful, mad Charlotte Corday 'made mincemeat of Marat in his bath.' Mincemeat indeed! The play reeked blood; the guillotine worked like fury; a cast of 300, many of them local unemployed, bayed with true revolutionary zeal; and in the end, half a

51

dozen heads including that of Robespierre were seen to be taken off. The crowds up in the gallery yelled for more.

Other productions at the Grand included shipwrecks, earthquakes, railway collisions, explosions and the 'House Full' notices went up every time. When *The Streets of Brighton*, a lurid drama based on Dion Boucicault's *Streets of London* – there were also versions set in other major towns and cities – was played, despite the doubts of the critics, every seat was taken. Just as they were at Eastbourne Hippodrome, where in the 'Great Fire Scene' in *The Poor of New York*, the local fire brigade was called on stage to put out the flames with their hoses. And if these productions were not enough to play upon the emotions of the playgoers, there were the well-tried tear-jerkers – *East Lynne, The Two Orphans, Drink, The Silver King, Driven from Home. . .*

The melodramas and thrillers, the hiss and boo productions, faded away with the advent of the talking cinema. There was a brief revival in the 1950s. Tod Slaughter took *Sweeney Todd* and *Maria Marten* to the Eastbourne Hippodrome for two weeks in 1953 and played to full houses. The wonderfully named Slaughter, a man of great charm and kindliness, played his parts very much tongue in cheek. Described as 'our favourite ham actor', he no doubt relished the melodramatic roles which he had really made his own.

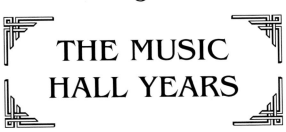

8

THE MUSIC HALL YEARS

Regency Brighton was a town of contrasts – in architecture and entertainment. The rich lived in elegant crescents of fine houses, the poor in narrow streets of tenements, lodging houses and beer shops. The rich flocked to the assembly rooms, the baths, the churches, to the wonder of the age, the Chain Pier; to the Theatre Royal and to the few respectable song and supper rooms. The poor had the music halls.

On the east side of town, on the corner of Mighell Street and Edward Street, was a public house called the Globe. Behind it was an old circus amphitheatre and here Burton's Music Hall opened in 1852. It was connected to the Globe, for music hall and drink always went hand in hand, and the admission price ranged from twopence to sixpence. Price of entry to the Theatre Royal was one shilling to four shillings so it is easy to see why the poor went to Burton's where the Chairman led beery choruses of songs of boisterous vulgarity and there were performing dogs doing the cleverest tricks, negro tambourine players, conjurors and jugglers. But it was no place for a lady.

Burton's burned down in 1854 but was rebuilt and renamed the Sussex Music Hall. Throughout its subsequent career there were constant battles with magistrates over the licence and eventually the passageway between it and the Globe was blocked up. Finally, after ten years of struggle, another fire destroyed the Sussex. Another music hall, the Canterbury, opened in Church Street in 1859 and for ten years attracted good crowds. It had been converted from an old pub and could seat 500 at its downstairs tables set at right angles to the stage. The acts, sometimes spectacular and frequently engagingly coarse, certainly had to please, for the audiences were extremely intolerant of whatever fell

Oxford Theatre of Varieties became by turns the Empire, the Coliseum, the Court, the Dolphin, Her Majesty's and finally, before it was demolished in 1967, the Paris Continentale Cinema. *Photo: C Horlock.*

short of the standards they expected. But the acts which survived were often very good. Certainly some music halls were better conducted than others. One known as the Regent Tavern lost its licence after there were complaints that the singing and dancing had gone on at times until six in the morning.

In 1863 another music hall opened in New Street, not two doors from the Theatre Royal. This was the Oxford, run at first as an old-style music hall with a chairman. In 1888 it was modernised and the tables, formerly fixed at right angles to the stage, were replaced by tip-up seats facing the stage and refreshment was now taken outside the main auditorium. The Oxford introduced patrons to brilliant furnishings but despite such lavish provision, it could not sustain the opposition of the 2,000 seat Alhambra on the seafront. In July 1891 it closed and was reincarnated in August 1892 as the Brighton Empire.

However, in its day the Oxford attracted such great music hall stars as Dan Leno, loved throughout the country for his hilarious *Railway Guard*, his *Recruiting Sergeant* and his *Waiter* numbers; Little Tich, Harry Champion and Vesta Tilley. The *Sussex Daily News* was enraptured by Little Tich:

'No one can have any idea of the variety of steps until he has seen Little Tich's galvanic legs . . . He is far away the most marvellous dancer the stage knows. But any description of his movements is impossible.'

Even Nijinsky went to see Little Tich whenever he could. And the little man – only 4 feet 6 inches tall – was lionised on the continent.

The Alhambra in King's Road and on the corner of Great Russell Street opened in October, 1888, not a hundred yards away from the Grand Hotel. Despite its cramped frontage it could hold an audience of up to 2,000. The interior was exquisite. The walls were painted rose, cream and gold, the drapes peacock blue and the seats violet velvet. In the panelled ceiling were three circles of electric lights and inside each circle was a gas burner. It was stunningly elegant, luxurious beyond imagination and for twenty years it was Brighton's most popular hall but like many other halls it eventually had to close, to reopen as a cinema.

Most of the top performers appeared at the Alhambra. George Robey, the Prime Minister of Mirth, played his first panto role, Jack Lollabout in *Dick Whittington*, in this theatre. For his music hall act this King of

Low Comedy would appear in a frock coat, without collar or tie – a flat

bowler hat on his head. He would glare at his audiences when they laughed, especially when his material verged on the over-ripe. 'Desist' he would order. 'I am not here as a source of public flippancy. Let there be merriment but let it be tempered with dignity and the reserve which is compatible with the obvious refinement of our environment.' Off stage George Robey was one of the most conventional of men. He was respectable, serious, responsible and he made his views on humour clear. 'I prefer honest vulgarity', he said. 'Honest vulgarity is neither filth nor purity. It lies somewhere between the two'. He died in 1954, the year after he was knighted for services to the British theatre.

George Robey and, below, Marie Lloyd.

Marie Lloyd was a regular visitor to the Alhambra over the years. *Oh Mr Porter,* she sang and followed it up with *'Twiggy Vous?'* – and one supposes that even those with no French twigged.

When the Empire opened in Pelham Place in Hastings in April, 1899, Marie Lloyd was top of the bill. To a resounding reception, the young woman whose father had once owned the Royal Albion Hotel in the town, sang four songs. Two of these were certainly suggestive. In addition to *Hallo, Hallo, Hallo* and *Everything in the Garden's Lovely*, she sang *I Wanted to See How it Felt* and *Bathing,* the last song posing the question, 'should the sexes bathe together?' This was certainly appropriate to Hastings where there was earnest debate on the council about the propriety of mixed bathing which, two years later, was to be allowed at the neighbouring highly respectable resort of Bexhill. With the top of the bill entertainers were the supporting acts – the unicyclists, acrobats, dancers, roller skaters, magicians and the strong men. There was George Hackenschmidt, wrestler and strong man, taking on all comers on stage just as the black boxer, Peter Jackson, did.

Another strong man was the Great Sandow, the Monarch of Muscle, who could lift a bar-bell weighing 500lbs at the same time supporting an iron-framed piano, a pianist and two vocalists.

Dan Sullivan could lift a baby elephant with his teeth and sever thick chains with his hands. Another muscle man, Apollo, regularly lifted 250lb sacks of flour over his head with one hand and strength was not an exclusively male attribute. Among many female strong arm artistes was Victorina, billed as 'the strongest woman in the world'. When she appeared at the Grand, Brighton, she picked up a 500lb weight and four attendants, two under each arm.

The Brighton Aquarium, a curious hybrid of a place established partly to satisfy the Victorian appetite for scientific information and partly to offer entertainment, was also in the music hall tradition. Its seats were not raked and its stage was small. It never matched Brighton's other theatres with their famous top of the bill acts but featured instead a

The wonders of the Aquarium were on occasions complemented by the presence of the celebrated Mohawk Minstrels. They were certainly there in 1894, as the poster on the right of the entrance shows. *Photo: C Horlock.*

variety of strange turns, among them mind readers and trampoline acrobats, budgerigar handlers, trick cylists and human hairpins. There were performing parrots and 'Educated Canines', Louis Lavater turned somersaults and played the violin simultaneously and Don Pottos, the 'World Renowned One-legged Spanish Dancer', performed his *Dance Avec Manteau*.

There are hints here of desperate acts and desperate managers but the great Mohawk Minstrels performed at the Aquarium and in 1891 Lottie Collins sang *Ta-ra-ra-boom-de-ay*, accompanying it with an outrageous high kicking dance. She went on to make a fortune touring the country with her English can-can, but she found money was not everything. She was even hissed by an audience in 1896 because she would not give them *Ta-ra-ra-boom-de-ay*. She was sick of it, she said, and no doubt physically exhausted as well with all that high kicking night after night.

Oh, how the audiences – and the errand boys – loved the songs they sang. *If You Were the Only Girl in the World, The Man Who Broke the Bank at Monte Carlo, Two Lovely Black Eyes* . . .

By the turn of the century music hall was coming to the end of its shelf life. In 1912 two factors hastened its demise – an Act of Parliament which prohibited the serving of food and alcoholic drink in auditoriums and the introduction of a Royal Command Performance which had the effect of making music hall more genteel. Marie Lloyd, one of the most popular of artistes, was not invited to appear for fear that the amiable vulgarity of her songs would not be acceptable. From now on the winks and nudges, the innuendo, the coarse-grained songs would be toned down. The seaside postcard quality of many performers would no longer be good enough. Although some carried on the old tradition – and Max Miller was undeniably the best known inheritor of a type of theatre he had never known at first hand – music hall changed into variety and no longer catered for the working class. The last nail in its coffin came in 1914 when its traditional audience lit their fags and marched off to Flanders with a cheerful enough music hall type of song:

'Goodbye-ee, goodbye-ee,
Wipe the tear, baby dear, from your eye-ee,
Though it's hard to part, I know
I'll be tickled to death to go . . .

9

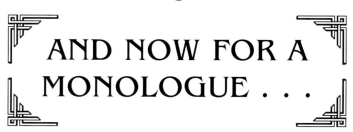

AND NOW FOR A MONOLOGUE . . .

It sounds so out of date now, the prose or poetic monologue. There are few reciters of verse any more and equally few who offer readings of the works of great writers. However there was a time when the elocutionist was on call at masonic meetings and ladies' nights, offering bits and pieces of Shakespeare and Tennyson or perhaps some of those simple poems which told of courage in adversity, of the cruelty of fate, of suffering nobly born, of heart wrenching tragedy and pathos and of the Englishman's code of honour.

It was on the halls where these monologues were most frequently heard, spoken or sung to background music by the likes of Albert Chevalier and later by their most important exponent, Bransby Williams, 'the Hamlet of the Halls'. He recited not only huge chunks of Shakespeare and Dickens but gave solo performances of *The Bells* and the *Transformation of Doctor Jekyll into Mr Hyde*. His repertoire of more than a hundred dramatic monologues included *The Whitest Man I Know; The Shooting of Dan McGrew; Christmas Day in the Workhouse;* and the most famous of all, *The Green Eye of the Little Yellow God*.

In a career which lasted from 1897 until 1960, Bransby Williams entranced his audiences by his lightning changes of costume and make-up. He would sit on the blacked-out stage, his back to the audience, lit by a single spotlight. They would see him putting on a wig, adding liner to his brows, powdering his face, and then he would stand up, still with his back to the audience and put on a jacket, a scarf, a hat. When he turned there was the wicked Mr Hyde or the vicious Bill Sykes; or a benevolent Mr Pickwick or Ebenezer Scrooge – or perhaps he would appear in a brass-buttoned tail coat with black knee breeches to declaim in clear, resonant tones some soliloquy from Shakespeare. Bransby Williams was a handsome man and a highly popular performer. He made frequent visits to the Alhambra and the Aquarium at Brighton and he appeared many times at Eastbourne, Hastings and Worthing. In 1954, for one week in June at the White Rock, he appeared in *Twinkle*.

His most popular monologue – the tale of a young officer, Mad Carew, who pays with his life to get his colonel's daughter the birthday present she requested – begins and ends:

There's a one eyed yellow idol to the north
of Khatmandu,
There's a little marble cross beneath the
town,
And a broken hearted woman tends the
grave of Mad Carew
While the yellow god for ever gazes down.

Billy Bennett.

This kind of monologue was ripe for parody after the First World War and Billy Bennett was the one to do it. *The Tightest Man I Know* replaced *The Whitest Man I Know* and in the place of *Christmas Day in the Workhouse* – a sincere diatribe against the indignities of the old workhouse system – came the comic monologue about army life and a hated sergeant major. *Christmas Day in the Cookhouse* concludes:

May the patent expire on your evening dress shoes,
May your Marcel waves all come uncurled,
May your flannel shirt shrink up the back of your neck
And expose your deceit to the world.
And now that I've told you my story
I'll walk to the clink by the gate –
And as for your old Christmas pudden,
Stick that on the next fella's plate.

Billy Bennett, billed as 'Almost a Gentleman', made a hit with these travesties of the old favourites. He was, between the wars, one of the most popular of comedians, appearing on stage in an ill-fitting dress suit and hob-nailed boots. Never smiling, he bellowed his material in the soberest manner, an old fashioned figure with a false Old Bill walrus type moustache and a quiff plastered across his brow. A bass drum in the orchestra pit would beat boom-boom at the conclusion of each verse or telling couplet.

In his take-off, *The Green Eye of the Little Yellow Dog*, Fat Carew gives his tie to his lady friend. For no explained reason – and in the world of the Bennett monologue there is no place for reason – she fixes the tie to the dog's tail with Carew's tie pin. The dog, seeking revenge, places his mistress's false teeth in Carew's bed. The concluding verse was always hysterically received:

> There's a cock-eyed yellow poodle to the north of Gongapooch,
> There's a little hot-cross-bun that's turning green,
> There's a double-jointed wop-wop doing tricks in who-flung-dung,
> And you're a better man than I am, Gunga Din.

Sometimes after he has invaded and occupied the stage, dressed in oversized boy scout trousers, his hat surmounted by a Union Jack and with an assemblage of pots, pans, the leg of a shop-window model and other irrelevant impedimenta about his waist, Ken Dodd will sing – or try to sing for he will constantly interrupt himself – *The Road to Mandalay*. He inherited this from Bennett, a fellow Liverpudlian and one of his great heroes. It runs:

> There's a farm on the horizon,
> Looking eastward to Siam;
> We could have some ham and eggs there,
> If they had some eggs and ham!
> But they've only got one hen –
> They call her Mandy, by the way -
> But they've found out she's a cock;
> That's why they can't make Mandy lay!

Among other fine comic monologuists to play the theatres and pier pavilions of the Sussex coast from the 1920s were Stanley Holloway with the various adventures of *Albert and the Lion* and *Sam Small*, the soldier who fought at Waterloo, Cyril Fletcher with his *Odd Odes*, Arthur Askey, the Western Brothers and Flanders and Swann.

10

. . . AND SOME MAGIC

There has been a significant number of great stage magicians, especially since the formation of the Hall of Magic in London in 1873 by the Maskelynes. And they have, some of them, been dogged by tragedy. Two of the greatest died on stage and another was involved in one of the great theatrical tragedies.

At the Oxford Music Hall, Brighton on 27 December 1881, Ali Ling Look, the Great Chinese Salamander, Lord of Fire, Cannon and Sword, had thrust walking sticks and swords down his throat and swallowed a dozen hard-boiled eggs. Towards the end of his act, after a series of dramatic pauses and rolls on the drums and the tinkling of Chinese cymbals, Ling Look's wife, who acted as his assistant, took a red-hot iron from a stove at the rear of the stage. She touched the iron with a piece of paper which instantly flared up; she then placed it in a bowl of water which hissed and steamed. Next she ran another iron, fresh from the stove, along Ling Look's forearm. Remarkably, it appeared to have no effect. Even more remarkably, he then chewed off two pieces of the metal. Next, he drank boiling oil. Then was to come the *pièce de resistance*. The chairman, for the Oxford was a traditionally-run music hall, called for silence, explaining that the Great Chinese Salamander needed to concentrate for the climax of his act.

Ling Look, graceful in his mandarin robes, went to the back of the stage where, resting on two stands, stood a small cannon made of wood and bound with brass. Crouching under the cannon, he swallowed another sword up to its hilt to which was attached a piece of string. The string from the sword hilt was attached to the cannon. Next his assistant poured gunpowder down the cannon's muzzle, ramming it down the barrel with a wad of paper. The trick was obviously to fire the cannon and thus dramatically jerk the blade from Ling Look's stomach. Taking yet another sword he raised the miniature cannon on the sword hilt. The barrel swept the auditorium. There was another roll on the drums, more tinkling of cymbals. On one knee Ling Look aimed the cannon at the dome of the ornate ceiling. Now his wife took another red-hot iron, placing it over the barrel. The cannon's elevation was slightly adjusted. Another pause, another small adjustment. Then the iron was applied to the touchhole. There was an explosion and the sword flashed into view, up from Ali Ling Look's throat. He stood up triumphantly, his arms outstretched for applause; the audience clapped and cheered and cheered. But then almost imperceptibly, the other sounds intruded, driving out the acclamation, silencing the applause.

The eyes of the pair on stage turned to the gallery. For up there, there was uproar. A member of the audience, a fifteen year old boy, George Smythe, had had his skull shattered. His blood and brains had splashed those around him and those below. He had been shot by Ali Ling Look. The performer was arrested and charged with killing the boy. At the inquest it was revealed that Smythe had been hit by the wad of paper that Ling Look's wife had rammed down the barrel.

At Lewes Assizes in January 1882, Ling Look was acquitted of manslaughter. The jury accepted that the trick had been rehearsed and performed previously and that there had been no indication of danger to the public.

Another of the great favourites on the variety stage was Chung Ling Soo, apparently Chinese but in reality an American. Billed as the World's Greatest Conjuror, he appeared at the Alhambra and also at the Hastings Hippodrome. He pulled live ducks from a boiling cauldron, swallowed lighted tapers, produced flowers from buckets. His most celebrated trick was intended to represent an execution by firing squad. After loading a rifle with live bullets – or so it must have appeared – Chung Ling Soo, at the stake, caught the bullet on a plate. He was killed on stage at Wood Green Empire in 1918, performing the trick which so mystified his audiences. In fact, the rifle had a false barrel into which the live round passed as a blank was fired. By sleight of hand, Chung Ling Soo then produced the bullets on the plate. Tragically, unlike his performances in Sussex, this time something went fatally wrong.

Carl Hertz, the King of Cards, played at the Aquarium when he was quite young. He was on the bill with Marie Lloyd at the opening of the Marine Palace of Varieties (later called the Hippodrome) at Hastings in 1899 and he claimed to be the first to present the Indian Rope Trick on the stage although Horace Goldin made a similar claim.

The Great Lafayette, born a German but a naturalised American, toured with a large company of forty artistes and a menagerie which included a lion. He was a frequent visitor to Sussex. One of his tricks was to turn a woman into a bag of dust. Another illusion was to appear in the guise of a sculptor, wearing a voluminous cape and beret. After creating a figure in a frame, the sculptor simply stepped inside his cape and disappeared whereupon the figure came to life to reveal – Lafayette.

But his most famous illusion was *The Lion's Bride*. Lafayette, dressed as an Indian, appeared on stage, doing his utmost to win the favours of a white girl. Frustrated when she rejects him, he throws the girl into the cage at the back of the stage. In it, there is a live lion. At that moment the theatre lights go out – when they come on again seconds later the girl is in the clutches of the lion – but safe.

How the audiences loved this trick. Does it spoil things to explain how it was done? Well, the lion's cage had two tiers. At first, the animal occupied the top one. As soon as the lights were extinguished, a slide was pulled out from under the lion's feet and it fell into the lower tier. In the dark, Lafayette, pulling on a lion skin, hurtled into the cage and when the lights went up there was the lion with the girl in his grasp. But what if the slide had not worked? Would the girl have been in real danger? And would the illusionist have been equally endangered? And, anyway, what did the lion feel about being dropped from one tier to another twice nightly?

It was at Edinburgh Empire one night in May 1911 that Lafayette's flaming torch set fire to the drop curtains and great flames suddenly engulfed the stage part-way through an illusion. The audience was saved by the safety curtain – Lafayette and eight members of the cast died.

In 1905, The Handcuff King, Harry Houdini, pulled in some of the greatest ever audiences at Hastings Hippodrome. He was an experienced showman, alive to the importance of publicity. No sooner had he arrived in town, than he threw out a challenge to anyone to prevent his escape from locks, bolts, bars and chains. The newspapers carried accounts of his acceptance of a local man's challenge to shut him in a hamper restrained by locks, straps and ropes.

Did the great man escape in the scheduled time? Of course he did, just as easily as he released himself from the strait jacket into which he had been strapped by an attendant from a local asylum. His challenge to the Hastings police was rejected. No, they would not lock him in one of their cells. He had already escaped from handcuffs at Scotland Yard.

Houdini could escape from anything – from safes, from strong boxes, from fire and water. Nothing could restrain him. Well, perhaps that is not entirely true. Before he died in a Detroit hospital on Hallowe'en 1926, he promised to send back a message from the other side on the anniversary of his death. For the next fifty years devoted followers gathered in the hope of something but it was thought eventually that Harry Houdini's last great illusion was beyond even his powers.

The illusionist, Horace Goldin, appeared at the Grand, Brighton in 1928 when his act was described as 'England's Greatest Road Show.' Both his pianist and piano disappeared from the stage. Another man, standing in front of a cannon, disappeared when it was fired and then reappeared. A hole was bored through yet another man's body, a live bird was shot into a burning globe allegedly at a thousand miles per hour. It is claimed that it was on this programme the Indian Rope Trick was performed for the first time in Europe although Carl Hertz would deny this. But the *piece de resistance* was sawing a woman in half while her legs and arms were held by members of the public. During this act Goldin walked through her divided body. Or so those present believed.

Goldin died on 22 August, 1939, just as he was about to reveal a plan to make the British army invisible in the event of war.

11

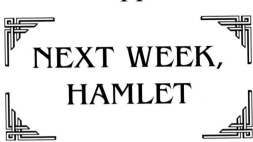

NEXT WEEK, HAMLET

Repertory companies produced, week in, week out, an inexorable chain of farces, thrillers, domestic dramas, classic tragedies and comedies, melodramas, post-West End hits and the inevitable pre-West End flop. Their strength was the loyalty they engendered in their regular patrons at Hastings, Worthing, Eastbourne and Bexhill. Brighton, too, had seasons of weekly repertory at the Palace Pier, the Grand Theatre and the Dolphin – formerly named the Empire, the Coliseum and Court – but theatres there tended more often to engage touring companies, preferably with prior-to-London productions.

Despite criticisms about the conveyor-belt quality of weekly rep productions there can be no denying the sheer hard work that went into the process. The actors themselves were always in rehearsal for the following week's show while appearing in seven or eight performances of the current production so it is hardly surprising that the plays were sometimes less than highly polished. Nevertheless, for many years the companies sustained themselves over demanding forty-week seasons. Harry Hanson, an erstwhile performer, had companies of Court Players in theatres round the country and one resident at Hastings from 1932 until the mid 1960s either on the pier – from 1955 'newly gas-heated for your winter comfort' – or at the White Rock Pavilion.

It is easy to condemn Hanson's choice of plays as cosy, trivial and trite but they were enjoyed in their day and the local press usually described them as 'charming' or 'refreshing,' or 'extremely amusing'. There was a whole range of frothy plays such as *Queen Elizabeth Slept Here; Is Your Honeymoon Really Necessary?; May I Borrow Your Wife?* ('the grand holiday laughter show'); and *A Bed for Two* interspersed with Ben Travers farces, Agatha Christie thrillers and the occasional powerful drama. In 1954 Hanson's company presented *The Age of Consent*, described as 'the story of working class people'. Advertisements warned: 'THIS PLAY IS NOT SUITABLE FOR CHILDREN.' Two years later, there were warnings that *Vice in the Street* was: 'SUITABLE FOR ADULTS ONLY.'

Repertory at Worthing was slower off the mark than at Hastings. In 1930 a couple of plays were put on at the Connaught Hall above a row

Bill Fraser.

of newly built shops in Chapel Street but there was little else to hearten the avid theatre goer. In the following year W Simson Fraser, better known as Bill Fraser, the actor who played Snudge in the TV series *Bootsy and Snudge*, put on some plays in the Ritz Ballroom. Then, with theatre manager Charles Bell, he went on to form the Mask Players and stage a weekly repertory of plays at the Connaught Hall. It was a production of *Pygmalion* in 1933 which established the company's reputation and popularity.

Two years later, and at a time when ever more new cinemas were being built throughout the country, the Swiss entrepreneur, Carl Seebold, decided to convert his Picturedrome in Union Place into a 900 seater theatre. It was given a new entrance and foyer in addition to a lounge and cocktail bar and the Mask Players moved from the old Connaught Hall to the new Connaught Theatre. With the outbreak of war the Connaught, like so manyb other places of entertainment throughout the country, was closed, only to reopen in 1941. For the next three years it housed a succession of touring shows and repertory companies and in 1944 the Rank Organisation took the lease and reintroduced weekly repertory with the Overture Players.

It was the Rank policy to train potential film actors in this company

68

and such promising newcomers as Christopher Lee, Diana Dors and June Whitfield came to Worthing to learn their trade. Commercial difficulties within the film industry obliged Rank to abandon this enterprise in 1950 but local businessmen, aware of how important the theatre had become to Worthing, took over the Connaught. For the next sixteen years it was an ornament to the town and to the theatrical profession.

Worthing Repertory Company

Lessees: Charles W. Bell & W. Simson Fraser
Licensee & General Manager: Charles W. Bell

PROGRAMME
PRICE TWO PENCE

New Connaught Theatre programme cover c1936.

In this period actors and actresses of major stature performed at Worthing. Among them were pre-war matinee idols Jack Buchanan and Bobby Howes, young Susannah York, the then unknown Patricia Routledge, and local boy Ian Holm. Among guest producers were Alan Ayckbourn, Peter Hall and Christopher Fry. At Bexhill plays were performed professionally by Philip Yorke's Country Players at the Kursaal from the mid 1930s. When that theatre closed Yorke and his company transferred to Egerton Park where, in spite of serious limitations of space, they pursued an ambitious programme of plays each summer season. The De La Warr Pavilion, which opened in 1935, was large enough to house extravagant shows and it quickly became the entertainment centre of Bexhill. National opera and ballet companies, orchestras under such great conductors as Sir Thomas Beecham and many top touring theatre companies graced its post-war summer seasons. In the winter months the resident repertory company would come in from the cold of Egerton Park to stage plays and a Christmas panto at the De La Warr. In 1950 the Century Players were succeeded by Richard Burnett's Penguin Players, a company which built up a loyal following with the usual crop of thrillers and farces, gentle comedies, dramas and the occasional classic.

Eastbourne's Devonshire Park Theatre with its twin Italianate towers and its cream stucco walls, is a building of distinct elegance. Frank

Bexhill's De La Warr Pavilion was the first public building in the country to have a welded steel frame. Below is Eastbourne's Devonshire Park Theatre.

Benson's Company were visitors in the early years of the century; Sir Phillip Ben Greet brought Shakespeare on several occasions as did Charles Doran's Company.

From 1906, under the direction of Murray King and Charles Clark, and later of other professional managements, the Devonshire Park was open all the year round and was able to attract sufficiently large audiences, even in winter, to make the theatre profitable for the next fifty or so years.

Patrons became accustomed to seeing well-produced plays, acted by the resident company, often with guest artists, interspersed with pre-London or post-London tours with leading ladies of the calibre of Dame Sybil Thorndike, Marlene Dietrich, Athene Seyler, Evelyn Laye and Margaret Lockwood.

Not that the demanding and often tart critic of the *Eastbourne Gazette* was always satisfied. She described Anna Neagle as 'the first lady of the ever-so-English screen' and the play in which she starred as 'yet another light comedy with its one interior set, small cast, and appeal to the box office – if not the intelligence – that is on its way to the West End'.

Margaret Lockwood in a scene from Peter Whelan's *Double Edge* at the Devonshire Park Theatre in 1976.

In 1965, when the resident rep was Richard Burnett's Penguin Players, a company which had moved over from Bexhill some years earlier, they were planning to offer, according to the *Eastbourne Gazette* – 'With an eye on the box office and in the sure knowledge that this is what holiday audiences want . . . a well-tried recipe of murder and comedy during this year's summer season'.

But it was a recipe that did not please the holidaymakers that year, or in the years that followed. The popular thriller, *The Late Edwina Black*, played to an audience of only thirty seven on the first night and the following week there was 'a small audience' for Wilde's classic comedy *An Ideal Husband*.

The decrease in repertory theatre audiences was being experienced nationally as well as locally but the *Gazette,* in 1966, felt confident enough to claim that 'from every viewpoint the live theatre industry in Eastbourne is very much alive'. Weekly rep did continue for a few more years at the Devonshire Park Theatre after the arrival of Charles Vance in 1969. But in the end, all along the coast, economic forces, audience indifference and the rival attraction of television brought the curtain down on a forcing ground of talent which had been of huge benefit to the British theatre.

12

HIGH KICKS, SMILES AND BODY STOCKINGS

Where are they now those ranks of chorus girls, all spangles and feathers, long, long legs and dazzling smiles – the Grosvenor Girls, the Tiller Girls, the Bluebell Girls before they left for France, the Six Clarkson Rosebuds, Sandy Powell's Eight Starlights and countless other troupes? Their names are now forgotten but not their precision, their high kicks and the cheery wave of the last girl as the chorus line danced off stage right.

They were at Hastings with Marie Lloyd, calling themselves Tiller's Eight Fairy Dancers. And when the Great Macdermott was at the Alhambra, he had the Mlle Lucelle ballet. And at the Aquarium Fred Wright's 'Specially Selected Company in their New and Wildly Whimsical Burlesque Extravaganza in Three Doses (to be taken at each performance)' had the Rochelle Ballet Troupe of Eight Dancers.

The ballet was always well represented in all the theatres and there was usually a ballet spot in the pantomimes too. The major companies put on ballet only a few months of the year and therefore to keep them afloat the dancers were obliged to appear in music halls and variety theatres, often with condensed versions of the classical ballets. So the great Pavlova appeared after the First World War in the theatre at the end of Brighton's Palace Pier as well as at the Royal Concert Hall in Hastings. Alicia Markova and Anton Dolin performed at Eastbourne in 1936 and during and after the Second World War a whole range of companies, among them Sadler's Wells, the Ballet Rambert and the Russian Ballet, appeared in most of the resorts.

It was in 1902, the American Maud Allen, a classical dancer, shocked the nation with her interpretation of the dance of Salome. 'Outrageous'

The Hazel Hastings Girls, one of the many chorus lines who tap danced their way across the stage of resort theatres all over the country.

was the verdict. 'Immoral,' others pronounced. 'House Full,' declared the billboards outside the theatres. In the same year Mlle Diane de Fontenay appeared at the Alhambra in a *tableau vivant* and the *Brighton Herald* was not shocked at all. In fact, it acknowledged her striking poses approvingly. 'This attractive lady,' says the report, 'has on many previous occasions drawn crowded audiences by exhibiting to them, in statuesque poses, a form which a kind Nature has endowed with all that one admires as ideal beauty in a woman'.

Mlle de Fontenay was accompanied by several other ladies who posed with her in a series of what were described as 'tasteful tableaux.' In *The Lady's Fan,* for example, she posed motionless (by law, incidentally, she might lose her licence should she move deliberately), as if made of white ivory. It has been suggested that Mlle de Fontenay – and her ladies, too, for that matter – was heavily covered in lacquer. If she wore a body-stocking, the journalist was unaware of it. As far as he was concerned, she wore no more than a narrow scarf, her body representing the fan handle.

From there came 'a gorgeous spread of feathers, ablaze with many-hued electric lights. Then she is a dragonfly spreading out gauzy bejewelled wings.' Quite a spectacle. And, by the way, the Alhambra had a good reputation as a place to which respectable ladies might be taken without fear of offence or embarrassment. As with so many of these acts, the public was advised that the ladies performed 'for art's sake.' So that was all right.

Brighton enjoyed many a show in which there were nude females. In 1930 Signor Arvi's Sparkling Revuesque Show came to the Grand. Arvi, an Englishman, was primarily an illusionist but then nude shows were themselves, for the most part, illusion. In this show he seemed to produce scantily clad girls almost at will. The programme proclaimed:

'There is nothing whatsoever between these beautiful female figures and the audience. No screens are drawn, no cabinets are closed, the figures move not. Some of the most beautiful living women are introduced in the flesh'.

Certainly the figures did not move but did they appear in the flesh? That is a doubtful claim. The 'delightfully daring' Driena at the same theatre in March 1942 posed principally at the back of the stage under subdued and selective lighting, offering tableaux under arty titles such as *September Morn, Peace and Beauty* and *Beauty Unadorned*. Like others in her trade she usually wore spangles strategically placed and often a flesh-coloured body stocking. At times gauze hangings were raised, one by one, in a kind of seven veils-ish style. But then, just at the climax the lights would go out. Cheating? Well, the punters did not complain.

The nude revue came into its own in the 1940s and early 1950s. Young men away from home, in military barracks, in strange towns, felt free to go to the kinds of show their mothers and wives would have forbidden had they remained at home. Peaches Page, Peaches Weston, Phyllis Dixey, Rosemary Andree were simply names that until then most of them had come across only in the newspapers. Perhaps they had read that Dixey had fallen foul of the Lord Chamberlain again, something to do with her fan or her chiffon, that the acts of the others did not conform with the requirements of some or other outraged Watch Committee, perhaps the black-outs were not quick enough. Maybe they thought that Jane was simply a cartoonist's creation in the *Daily Mirror*. And now, with the war, all of these young warriors were free to go to see these

Beauty in a body stocking? The strippers had to stand absolutely still. Any movement and the Lord Chancellor could close the show. *Photo: C Horlock*

goddesses. Even Jane had had life breathed into her. Christine Leighton-Porter, who had been artist Norman Petts' model for his strip cartoon in the *Mirror,* made personal appearances, topping the bill in 'girlie' shows throughout the country.

It was a hard enough job for the strip teasers. It was not enough simply to look beautiful, sexy, slinky, provocative. They had to remain absolutely still on stage. Tiring work when they had to stand as Venus de Milo for an achingly long time and they often longed for a black-out which enabled them to change to the next pose.

Phyllis Dixey, the Peek-a-Boo girl, born Selina Tracy in Wales, was the acknowledged Queen of Strip. Her career began in the 1930s but her act was given an enormous boost by the war. Looking gloriously innocent, although clearly it must have been a sexy sort of innocence, she was neither crude nor suggestive. 'Disrobing with decorum' might have been an apt description of her act. And she had a sly wit, too, if one goes by her comment on stage on one occasion. Referring to an early encounter with an agent, she told her audience in her soft voice: 'I failed my first audition. I could not sing in that position.'

Dixey appeared at Brighton Hippodrome and at Bognor where she broke local box office records in 1946. In the following year at the

Devonshire Park Theatre in Eastbourne she played the lead in a comedy, *Marry or Burn,* which the local newspaper reviewed approvingly. In June 1948, she paid another visit to Eastbourne, this time to the Hippodrome in *Peek a Boo*, a revival of the wartime revue in which she had been so successful.

The supporting acts for Dixey's show included *Pharaoh's Amorous Maidens, The Varga Models* and *Phyllis Dixey's Ballet Parisienne.* Another member of the cast, the exotic Paula Lennard, performed an extravagant snake-like dance but the star was undoubtedly Phyllis Dixey.

Also playing in the town that week was Sandy Powell in *Star Wagon* at the Pier Theatre and Clarkson Rose's *Twinkle* at the Devonshire Park Theatre. Needless to say, in those days of holidays taken at the English seaside, each of the shows played to full houses.

There was a significant change of taste in entertainment after the war and Eastbourne reflected it by booking many so-called 'girlie' shows. At the Hippodrome in 1948 the bill was topped by three performers:

Bathing beauty contests were another sure-fire crowd puller. These girls are competing for the title of Holiday Princess at Butlin's, Saltdean.

77

Sirdani, the comedy magician with the catch phrase, 'Don't be fright'; Albert Whelan, the immaculate veteran Australian, best known for being the first performer with a signature tune which he whistled as he languidly peeled off his white gloves, folded his white silk muffler and placed his top hat and cane on a side table; and Rosemary Andree, the blonde with the perpetual grin, described as 'Britain's Pocket Venus,' who presented an act entitled *Confessions of a Cover Girl* which allowed her to appear in a series of nude poses.

At the Grand, Brighton in 1951, Gerda Jordan presented 'attractive poses' in a show called *The Girls are Back*. Other shows at this time at the Hippodrome included *1001 Folies* featuring Karina 'who dances in amazing fashion'. Another production, *Don't be Shy, Girls*, included a nudist colony scene with poses by three exotic French models, Mignonne, Marlene and Estelle, and Apache dancers Andre and Eva Gamon were there to perform their 'rip-tease' dance.

A number of the shows had French titles. There was *Une Nuit de Montmartre; Soir de Paris* and *A la Carte* with Davy Kaye, although of the first there was said to be nothing French or salacious; of the second that it was not French in either its material, its presentation or its artistes; and the third was described as being about as French as a Chelsea bun.

These kinds of shows – and there were many of them up and down the country – were often tired old productions with a couple of speciality acts, a comedian and stooge, a musical act, a singer and a gaggle of chorus girls to open each half and come on dancing the can-can in the final production number. And somewhere there would be a nude. Despite the promise suggested by their titles, French this, French that, they could not save variety. They all had something in them to titillate their audiences but they failed.

But we cannot blame the French.

The truth is that variety was nearing its end. And the 'girlie show' was simply an attempt to rescue it. But, as one theatre barmaid said at the time:

'Nudes. That's what has killed the business. Who wants to take their children to see girls undressing?"

Well, why not leave the kids at home?

78

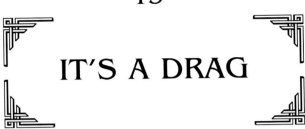

13

IT'S A DRAG

Men dressing as women has always been a feature of the English stage. This in part accounts for the lasting popularity of *Charley's Aunt* which must have been played on countless occasions by both amateur and professional companies. Of course we know from the outset that we are watching a man dressed as a woman. We are in on the plot even if some of the characters are not. It all adds to the fun.

Then there are the great dames of pantomime and those particularly renowned in Sussex included Clarkson Rose, hailed by some as the First Dame of the British Empire; Jack Tripp, a brilliantly eccentric dancer and another of those with claims to be one of the finest dames; and of course, Douglas Byng, who refused to play the role as a humble widow but insisted on being majestically attired as a real lady such as Alderman Fitzwarren's widow. Arthur Lucan as Old Mother Riley, that absurd Irish washerwoman with the flailing limbs and the equally uncertain grip on language, never played panto in Sussex but he did bring his show to Brighton, Eastbourne and Hastings where as ever he was a sure-fire hit with both children and adults. Norman Evans, the northern *Over the Garden Wall* comic, enjoyed two excellent seasons in Eastbourne and also made several appearances in other Sussex theatres.

However, several highly successful post-war shows were somewhat different. The casts were composed exclusively of ex-servicemen dressed as women and with the difference that they were extremely glamorous, it no longer being apparent that they were men. Some of the shows toured for several years. These included *Soldiers in Skirts*, the longest running of these shows, which came to the Brighton Grand and to Eastbourne Hippodrome. Despite the all-male casts, they produced convincing looking female nudes. Other shows were *Forces in Petticoats*, *Desert Rats* and *Hurrah for the Sea*. In 1947 the Hippodrome presented *This Was the Army* in which, said the bills, 'the most feminine looking member of the cast is undoubtedly Sonny Dawkes who not only looks and speaks but sings like a woman'. The woman he sang like, as a matter of fact, was the American film actress, Deanna Durbin. No raised eyebrows here. Presumably the audience took it all as a jolly fine take-off of a woman. Certainly it was a highly popular show. It was presented several times in the 1950s at the Regal in St Leonards.

In 1948, the Hippodrome at Eastbourne presented *We Were in the Forces* in which three of the cast were billed as 'almost a lady', 'some lady' and 'the perfect lady'. *Forces Showboat* was the best and classiest of the army drags. Here 'the surprise turn of the show' was the young Swansea comedian, Harry Secombe, who had been heard on the radio in *Variety Bandbox*. He dared to perform his shaving act which was better received in Eastbourne than it had been in Bolton where the theatre manager had paid him off prematurely. 'You're not shaving in my bloody time,' Secombe had been told.

It was in one of the productions of this show that the antics of the cast, some of whom insisted upon continuing with their female personae off stage, persuaded Danny La Rue to quit the drag show circuit. He had appeared in *Showboat, Soldiers in Skirts* (Danny Carroll is in small print on the bill above*)* and *Forces in Petticoats* but was always keen, when the show was over, to become Danny Carroll once more. It was never his wish to be other than a male entertainer who chose, solely for stage purposes, to wear drag. He is a man who creates an illusion of a beautiful woman but it is a joke and with his gruff 'Wotcher, mates', he makes it plain that it is a man in the extravagant dress, behind the exquisite make up – a man who has those so lovely legs.

In the early 1950s, both Brighton and Eastbourne welcomed *Kiss me Goodnight, Sergeant Major* and *This was the Army,* the latter then in its seventh year and for which the bill proclaimed 'Every Beautiful Miss is a Perfect Gentleman'.

Both were highly polished shows, extravagantly dressed with first class production standards and extremely costly to stage. This was a factor that led to the decline of the spectacular drag shows. By the mid-1950s they no longer had a place on theatre bills.

Rex Jameson, who appeared many times in theatres in Sussex as Mrs Shufflewick, was a highly regarded post-war performer. She – it is best to

Danny La Rue 'creating the illusion of a beautiful woman'.

recall Jameson by his stage name – would stagger from the wings, always just slightly the worse for drink – an absurd figure in a drab grey costume and wearing a hat with a single feather. The essentially genteel Mrs Shufflewick was not a stage drunk act; she was simply a character who, under the influence, unbent and became, as Jameson described her, 'broadminded to the point of obscenity,' one of her obsessions being sex. She would confide her secret to the audience that she was a former variety stage performer. As Bubbles Latrine with her Educated Sheepdogs, she claimed to have had her successes and her excesses.

Mrs Shufflewick's confidences were as frank as the period allowed

Transformation scene – Vesta Tilley in male and female attire.

but were they such a far cry from the events in the Duke Street Theatre in Brighton in 1793? That year's sensation was the Chevalier D'Eon, a celebrated figure in the town, who fenced with a Guards officer from one of the regiments stationed locally. Those who were fortunate enough to gain entry to the theatre and to occupy the highly priced seats had little patience with the play which preceded the encounter. They probably also paid less attention to D'Eon's brilliant swordplay than to ascertaining whether they were watching a male or female. D'Eon appeared in 'a blue satin shape, a white satin petticoat, and a large helmet, decorated with a plume of white feathers, which gave her, or him, a formidable but somewhat droll aspect.'

There have, of course, been countless women dressed as men on stage. Among the most celebrated was Vesta Tilley who, dressing as an Edwardian 'masher', with topper, gold knobbed cane and cigar, sang *Burlington Bertie*, *After the Ball* and *Algy, the Piccadilly Johnnie*. She was regularly on theatre bills at Brighton, Bognor and Hastings. At

Eastbourne's Devonshire Park Theatre in August 1916 she appeared dressed as a Tommy, singing:

'I joined the army yesterday,
So the army of today is all right.'

After months of the most ghastly bloodletting, the British public seemed still not to realise what was happening just across the Channel. On another occasion, at the Royal Command Performance, Queen Mary and the ladies accompanying her refused to look at Tilley, a woman in man's clothing, although this did nothing to hinder her career as a firm favourite of the halls. She was the 'matchless' Vesta, a consummate artist with a wonderful stage presence. In spite of her subject matter and her costume, her femininity always shone through.

Hetty King, a long-lived performer who appeared at Eastbourne as late as the 1960s, often came on stage dressed as a guardsman or a slightly inebriated gent, but her most popular impersonation was of a sailor, taking out his penknife, cutting his quid of tobacco, filling his pipe and striking a match on the seat of his trousers before launching into *All the Nice Girls Love a Sailor* or one of the other songs of the day.

Other male impersonators who appeared on local stages included Millie Gold, billed as 'The Most Genuine Ideal Boy'; Maisie Holland, 'The female George Lashwood'; May Lilian Levey, 'The Handsomest Man on the Stage'; Little Dolly Dandy, 'The Pocket Vesta Tilley'; and Dolly Marney, 'The Perfect Boy'. These acts performed right until the last years of variety. The powerfully voiced Ella Shields, famous for *Burlington Bertie from Bow* – in contrast to Vesta's similarly-titled song – and *If You Knew Susie* and *Oh What a Difference the Navy's Made to Me*, was on the bill at the Regal, St Leonards in 1951.

14

VARIETY ADDS SPICE TO POST-WAR LIFE

There was no let-up in the entertainment industry during the war. Even though some theatres were closed there was work for actors and comedians and singers entertaining the troops and those engaged on work of national importance wherever they happened to be. The BBC produced a wide range of comedy and variety shows like *Workers Playtime, Round the Horn* and *Much Binding in the Marsh* which kept many of the old time favourites, singers and comedians in work.

Robb Wilton had topped the bill over many years. 'The day war broke out' was the line with which he opened his act throughout the war and it endeared him to the nation. The careers of Tommy Handley, Richard Murdoch and Arthur Askey, Hetty King and Nellie Wallace and many others prospered.

Once hostilities were over a new wave of performers were waiting to find a place in the affections of the radio and theatre audiences. What is clear is that there was a strong public desire for new stars. And they came in great numbers in the succeeding years. Some of them were passing fancies but others are favourites yet.

It was through radio in many cases they made their first impact. Thus Frankie Howerd, appearing in 1947 at Brighton's Grand, was referred to as 'the Famous Comedian from *Variety Bandbox*', a popular programme which gave openings to several young artistes who were to make their names. Howerd made other sorties into Sussex. He did one night stands at Eastbourne, either at the pier or at the Hippodrome. He appeared in a play at Worthing's Connaught Theatre and was a great favourite of Brighton audiences.

It was in this period that the Grand in particular gave opportunities to other rising talents. Harry Secombe, another *Variety Bandbox* performer, and Spike Milligan appeared there on the same bill in 1947, both being described, with some accuracy, as 'infectiously lunatic.'

Norman Wisdom at the outset of his career was billed as 'The Successful Failure'. After less than three years in the business he was top of the bill at the Hippodrome at Eastbourne and he was described as 'always riotously amusing'. In 1957 he was the guest star at Sandy Powell's one thousandth performance on Eastbourne's pier and crowds lined the streets to welcome him.

Derek Roy appeared in the early post-war years at the Grand. At the time he was very popular – a performer of great wit and polish with his own programme, *Happy Go Lucky* – yet he was ultimately to fade.

In 1947 the Grand also gave opportunities to Max Bygraves, 'Britain's Laziest Comedian', so called because of the relaxed manner he continued to project in his act. In the following year Tommy Cooper was to make a strong impression on the Grand's audiences with his eccentric magic act.

At the White Rock Pavilion in

Two of the 'rising talents' from radio's *Variety Bandbox*, Frankie Howerd and, below, Harry Secombe.

85

Hastings other new stars were on show. In 1950, Peter Sellers, the BBC's new 'star impressionist' was there. Reg Dixon, top of the bill in the 1949 *Fol de Rols,* came back in 1950 as a solo turn. At the De La Warr, Bexhill in 1950 Beryl Reid, described as 'Radio's Comedy Girl', from *Educating Archie* – another forcing bed for comedians – was a huge success. It was at the same theatre and in the same year that Robert Moreton made a solo appearance. Of him the press was to say: 'No droll has raised more laughter recently than Moreton has with his *Bumper Fun Book'*. Like Tony Hancock he was to commit suicide in Australia.

In the early 1950s Hancock was in a concert party at Bognor. He appeared less successfully than several of his contemporaries in *Variety Bandbox.* Nevertheless he made it to radio and thence to to the Brighton Hippodrome and then to practically every other Sussex venue.

Norman Vaughan.

Norman Vaughan appeared in a show called *Evening Stars* at Worthing and in 1955 he was in *Twinkle* at the Pier Pavilion. Within a few years he would be an extremely popular compere of *Sunday Night at the London Palladium,* his catch word, 'Dodgy', finding its way into the nation's vocabulary.

Bruce Forsyth was at Eastbourne Hippodrome in Bernard Delfont's *Gaytime* in 1958. This was a rescue show after the previous season's indifferent offering, *Light up the Town,* with Graham Stark and Billy Burden. With the young Forsyth at the helm *Gaytime* was an unqualified success. At the conclusion of the first night's performance producer Hedley Claxton told the audience: 'If ever a star was born, there is one standing on this stage tonight'. It was, in fact, in the course of this show that he was called upon to take over as compere of *Sunday Night at the London Palladium.* If Bruce Forsyth has since then only rarely shown his undoubted talent and versatility, if he has tended to rely on being no more than a genial game show host, he has nevertheless demonstrated a staying power that has maintained his great popularity with the British public.

During the war there were several popular girl singers. Vera Lynn, 'a dainty girl with good looks and a good voice and a genuine feeling for the heart of a song', had appeared at Brighton Hippodrome and other venues when singing with the Ambrose Orchestra in which her husband to be, Harry Lewis, played the clarinet. Her poignant songs of separation and hope – *We'll Meet Again, The White Cliffs of Dover* – remained popular standards after the war and she became the first British artist to top the American Hit Parade with her recording of *Auf Wiederseh'n* which sold more than 12 million copies.

Vera Lynn, ' a dainty girl with good looks . . . '

Another wartime favourite was Anne Shelton who topped the bill at the Grand on its last night in 1955. *My Yiddishe Momma* was perhaps her best known song. Alma Cogan, who died young, had a wonderfully husky yet powerful voice. She appeared in panto at Worthing, her home town. The Grand at Brighton in 1947 had another budding star on the bill. This was Petula Clark, described as 'Britain's Premier Child Star'. By 1950, when she was at the White Rock Pavilion, Hastings, having appeared in the *The Huggetts* film series, she was billed as 'the famous J Arthur Rank star of film and radio'.

In 1948 Julie Andrews appeared in one of the Sunday evening shows at Eastbourne's Winter Garden as a soloist

Petula Clark.

Ice shows were costly to stage but extremely popular with the British public. Audiences sat with rugs round their knees to watch spectacular production numbers, comedy acts and to see world champion skaters go through their medal winning routines.

with Vic Oliver conducting the British Concert Orchestra. She was second on the bill and was described in the programme as 'A Sensational New Twelve Year Old Soprano.' Her range and power were deemed incredible for one so young and were said to be already of opera house quality. But her talent led her elsewhere, ultimately to Hollywood and *The Sound of Music* and other successful films.

Russ Conway, playing *Sidesaddle* and a string of other toe tapping tunes, and Frankie Vaughan, 'a young singing star who should go far,' were on the bill at the Grand in 1950. Vaughan topped the bill at the Brighton Hippodrome in 1958 and 1966.

In the 1960s it was plain that the end was approaching. The increasing costs of getting a variety show on the road, complete with orchestra, scenery and costumes, resulted in fewer and fewer

Russ Conway.

big productions with top names coming to the seaside resorts. Singers and comedians were finding that appearing on television, now in almost every home and since 1967 available in colour, was a much less arduous way of earning a living than barnstorming round the country year after year to entertain dwindling audiences. And the audiences had dwindled because the British public had discovered the package tour and was off by the coach and plane load to the Costa Brava to soak up the sun.

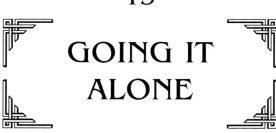

15

GOING IT ALONE

One-man and one-woman shows, placing so much responsibility on a performer in terms not only of acting but of choosing and organising material appropriately in the first place, seem to be a particularly courageous form of entertainment. In the years after the Second World War the prodigiously talented Welsh actor and playwright, Emlyn Williams; the equally gifted Irish actor and writer, Micheal MacLiammoir, co-founder with Hylton Edwards of the Gate Theatre in Dublin; and a 'typically English' star of stage, screen and radio, Joyce Grenfell, all appeared in Sussex theatres. While it was never difficult to describe Emlyn Williams and Micheal MacLiammoir as actors, the description of Joyce Grenfell as an actress always seems less appropriate. She always seemed to be participating simply for the fun of it and carried on to the stage an artlessness which might have been straight out of the Women's Institute, which was precisely the kind of impression she wished to give.

In 1951, Williams came to the Theatre Royal, Brighton. Alone on the stage he read a variety of excerpts from Dickens' works. Touring the country with this programme, much as Dickens had done ninety years earlier, Williams captured the same atmosphere. There was the simple reading desk; the arm rest; the ledge for the water jug and glass; and there for all to see, it seemed, was Dickens himself, fork-bearded, dark-suited, white-gloved, the voice measured and powerful.

The tour was repeated a number of times, playing at Bexhill in 1957. Emlyn Williams brought Dickens to the people just as Bransby Williams had been doing on variety bills for so many years. And he was also responsible for ensuring the popularity of the Welsh poet, Dylan Thomas, whose works he presented on a tour entitled *A Boy Growing Up* and which he brought to the De La Warr and Eastbourne Winter Garden in 1960. It was a performance of great fire and flourish and highly successful.

Joyce Grenfell Requests the Pleasure came to the White Rock Theatre in Hastings and Brighton's Theatre Royal in early 1954. Her programme comprised a series of amusing monologues and light songs. In the monologues, she created characters out of no more than intonation and mannerism. Her audiences were introduced to an infallibly optimistic kindergarten teacher – 'George, don't do that'; a housewife in church who began to fear, in the middle of Sunday service, that she had not turned off the cooker; a middle-aged woman singing at the Albert Hall but not able to concentrate fully.

CONGRESS THEATRE
EASTBOURNE
General Manager: George Hill

Harold Holt Ltd. present

An evening with

Joyce Grenfell

with
William Blezard
at the piano

Joyce Grenfell's characters were for the most part very southern English, middle class ladies with the occasional sprinkling of charladies and unsophisticated village women. They were females who suffered minor embarrassments at worst. There was no place for tragedy or high drama here. She might just introduce a touch of pathos but nothing stronger. Nevertheless, these were hugely enjoyable studies which brought her much acclaim.

In December 1960 Micheal MacLiammoir brought his programme of Wilde's works, entitled *The Importance of Being Oscar,* to the Winter Garden at Eastbourne, immediately after a triumphant production at the Apollo in London. The multi-talented MacLiammoir spoke, it is said, with a 'voice like fine claret'. He worked with a simple set, his only props being a writing table, period sofa, chair, decanter and glass. He selected from Wilde's work to illustrate different periods of the writer's life – what he described as the Happy Prince period, the Green Carnation period and the last years, *De Profundis*. MacLiammoir's performance was not really an impersonation but it was evident that he had both a deep sympathy for the man and admiration for his work. He rattled off Wilde's epigrams as if he had just coined them. It was a spellbinding performance and MacLiammoir was hastily engaged to return to Eastbourne for a repeat in the new year.

In the first half of the programme, MacLiammoir told of the life of young Oscar who had loved Lily Langtry, of his lecture tour of the USA, of giving a lecture about Benvenuto Cellini to the tough miners of Leadville whom he won over completely against all odds. It seems now to be an absurd location and topic. Whoever could have thought of putting the aesthete Wilde in such an arena? Yet, he had enthralled them. They liked the idea of Cellini. 'Why'n't you bring him widja?' they had asked. To bring the first half to a close, MacLiammoir read extracts from *Dorian Gray*. The second half was more sombre, dealing with Wilde's trial and imprisonment. Finally, he read from *De Profundis* and the *Ballad of Reading Gaol*. This was a towering performance.

In their own ways, all three performers gave towering performances.

16

MUSIC, MUSIC, MUSIC

There was a powerful appetite for good musical entertainment in the burgeoning seaside resorts of East and West Sussex – a desire which was satisfied by the formation of a number of locally-based orchestras. In today's infinitely wealthier society it is hard to imagine how such towns could possibly afford to employ full-time musicians for at least part of the year, or why they should choose to do so. Music of every kind is now available on air, screen, tape deck, turntable and CD at the click of a switch – you can even get it, like it or not, while told to 'hold' on the telephone.

But in the days when the Edison Bell phonograph was a marvel of modern science the residents of Bexhill, Eastbourne, Brighton, Hastings and Bognor did not have to rely on the reedy imperfections of its recordings. They could hear their favourite songs and symphonies first hand from their own municipal orchestras and choirs.

Brighton's accessibility to London, even before the arrival of the railway, not only made it attractive to visitors but also to those involved with the performing arts. The composer Rossini, on his first visit to England in 1823, had no hesitation in travelling along the coach road from the capital to the Royal Pavilion, where he was received in its magnificent music room by King George IV. Nor had Paganini, who gave a recital in the Assembly Room of the Old Ship four years later.

A Czech pianist and music teacher, William Kuhe, for thirty years provided the impetus to Brighton music. In 1869 he organised the first of a series of festivals 'on a scale never yet attempted in Brighton.' They continued until 1883, attracting musicians of international renown, and were a credit to the town of Brighton and to Kuhe's great vision and

The Kursaal at Bexhill was built in 1896 as the first stage of a pier that never materialised.

enterprise. But they never made money and plans for future, even grander, projects were abandoned.

Joseph Sainton, leader of the Brighton Municipal Orchestra, was successful in reviving the festival and engaging such distinguished composers as Edward Elgar, Edward German and Coleridge Taylor. But money continued to be a problem and Sainton, frustrated, resigned.

In later years there were attempts to revive the municipal orchestra but these ventures were short lived. Under that eminently capable musician, Jan Hurst, they ought to have succeeded but received little support from the local authority. When Sir Thomas Beecham conducted the orchestra he lavished great compliments upon its first class musicianship but condemned the acoustics of the Aquarium. Sir Henry Wood railed against the lack of publicity for his concerts and Elgar, then living at Brickwells in the West Sussex village of Fittleworth, publicly criticised the council and its entertainments committee. Only Herbert Menges, who founded the Brighton Philharmonic Players in 1925, had the staying power to provide fine accessible music to the public for the next forty years.

The provision of entertainment, and particularly music, at Bexhill rested upon the patronage of Viscount Cantelupe, later the eighth Earl De La Warr, and its quality derived from an Austrian musician and an English musician. It was Cantelupe's initiative which led to the building of the Kursaal, a pier-like structure juttting out to sea from the De La Warr Parade. If not entirely satisfactory, it was the only hall in the town large enough to accommodate orchestras and public.

It was also Viscount Cantelupe who first appointed Stanislaus Wurm, the Austrian violinist and former orchestra leader at the Imperial Hofburg Theatre in Vienna, to provide an orchestra for Bexhill. Thus came the introduction of the White Viennese Band, formed in 1894, an innovation so successful that the band – not all Austrians, despite the name – was appointed to play for the next five years, three of them in the newly built Kursaal, a name which must have sounded especially friendly to the conductor's ear and impressive to the locals who like many English at the time had a warm regard for most things Germanic. For such a comparatively small resort Bexhill's music provision was good. From 1906 there were daily concerts in the summer season at the Pergola, a partially covered open-air theatre in Egerton Park which was eventually rebuilt as the Egerton Park Theatre.

James Glover, Director of Music at Drury Lane from 1893 to 1922, lived in Bexhill and served as the town's mayor in 1906-1907 and as

James Glover seated, hat in hand, with his orchestra.

deputy mayor during the mayoralty of Lord Brassey the following year. It was through his influence that a number of famous musicians were persuaded to play at the Kursaal where, in a space of eight years, the energetic Glover promoted 2,000 concerts.

From 1911, there were outdoor concerts at the Colonnade, a popular centre for military bands as well as orchestral music until the building of the De La Warr Pavilion. Hundreds, sheltered by canvas screens and in an area illuminated in the evening by strings of coloured lights, listened to the military bands and to the Borand Paikin Orchestra which played there for many years.

After the 1939-45 war there was no attempt to revive a municipal orchestra. The Pavilion Trio played twice daily at the De La Warr Pavilion and there were concerts there throughout the year with such soloists as Richard Tauber, the great Austrian tenor and the piano duo, Rawicz and Landauer. Beecham conducted the Royal Philharmonic there in 1950 and later in the year the London Philharmonic gave a concert. There were lighter occasions too, with the immensely popular Luton Girls' Choir, the George Mitchell Choir with Semprini, Vic Oliver and the British Concert Orchestra and the jazz bands of Chris Barber and Johnny Dankworth.

Vic Oliver regularly presented programmes of both classical music and popular classics with the British Concert Orchestra at Hastings, Brighton and Eastbourne. He was a fine musician, having spent several years with the Graz Opera House orchestra as a violinist, and at the same time he was an extremely popular comedian with a faithful radio audience and much in demand in the variety theatre. But there was even more to the bow of this most interesting man. In his native Austria, he had been a cavalry officer and adjutant to a prince and, until they were divorced in 1950, he was married to Sarah Churchill, the actress daughter of Sir Winston Churchill.

Worthing had always been somewhat tentative about its music and even as late as 1934 the orchestra was modest in number. Under Herbert Lodge, however, its prestige grew and it made frequent broadcasts from the Pier Pavilion with distinguished soloists and conductors, among them Eric Coates and Sir Henry Wood. In the post-war period the employment of a full municipal orchestra proved too expensive for the council and in the 1950s it was reduced to an undeniably popular octet

Military band concerts in the Grand Parade bandstand have been a feature of Eastbourne's summer season. Playing here is the Band of the Royal Corps of Transport.

under the baton of James Kershaw but eventually even that proved too much of a burden for the public purse.

From the first grand concert in the Pavilion of the Winter Garden on July 5 1876 Eastbourne offered its residents and visitors some fine music. By the turn of the century the orchestra had fifty instrumentalists and, in the summer, when it was conducted by Norfolk Megone, it was called the Devonshire Park Grand Orchestra and in winter, when the conductor was Pierre Tas, it was the Duke of Devonshire's Orchestra.

The Eastbourne Municipal Orchestra achieved a significant degree of celebrity under the leadership of Theo Ward and later Captain Amers. Over the years many great names appeared in concerts with it at the Floral Hall, among them Pablo Casals, Dame Myra Hess, Alexander Glazounov, Edward Elgar, and the ubiquitous Thomas Beecham. Furthermore, in the course of each year, soloists such as Count John McCormack, Kreisler, and Moiseiwitsch were invited to sing and play with the orchestra. Between the wars the corporation engaged a smaller orchestra under Kneale Kelly and booked military bands to play in its handsome new seafront bandstand. In the 1950s and 1960s there were big band concerts in the Winter Garden – Jack Hylton, Ray Ventura and his Collegians, Billy Cotton and his band. The music was more modern, more brash, but brilliantly performed by first-class musicians.

When looking back on the Eastbourne music scene it is the broadcast concerts on Sunday nights 'from the Palm Court of the Grand Hotel' that everyone remembers. Albert Sandler and his Orchestra, with Jack Byfield at the piano, came to the Grand in 1925 and the concerts were relayed live from the Palm Court of the hotel until the war, during and after which they were recorded in the BBC's studios. Albert Sandler was succeeded by Tom Jenkins, who described the hotel's Palm Court lounge as 'easily the most perfect hall I have ever played in.'

Perhaps most readily associated with the BBC's post-war *Grand Hotel*

The Max Jaffa Trio with, l to r, Jack Byfield, Reginald Kilbey and Max Jaffa.

98

radio programmes was the Max Jaffa Trio of Jack Byfield, cellist Reginald Kilbey and violinist and conductor Max Jaffa. In the Palm Court of the Grand Hotel itself a dance band played from 1963 – an innovation not wholly to the liking of the majority of the older residents.

Towards the end of the nineteenth century one of the world's greatest violinists, Fritz Kreisler, appeared at the grandly named Royal Concert Hall in St Leonards – it later became the Elite cinema – as did Mark Hambourg, the pianist, Sousa and his great marching band and the Moore and Burgess minstrels. It was largely in response to public demand for a suitable hall for first class orchestral concerts, that the council built the White Rock Pavilion. Its opening in 1927 was marked by a four day music festival and this became an annual event with guest conductors and soloists of international stature. A regular winter series of concerts, often broadcast by the BBC, was established by conductor Basil Cameron and continued from 1931 by Julian Harrison.

For a while, during and after the war, the orchestras of Eastbourne and Hastings combined as the South Coast Philharmonic and played in both towns. This collaboration could not be sustained, however, because petrol rationing made travelling to rehearsals, and to concerts at different venues, too difficult.

'Star artists' – twenty of them – were offered by *Star Wagon* and Arthur Askey had the support of the *Twinkle* company at a radio guest night. Olive Fox and Clarkson Rose were the bill toppers for the show's 1953 Coronation edition.

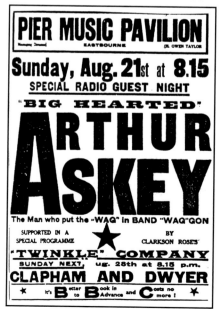

PIER MUSIC PAVILION
EASTBOURNE

Sunday, Aug. 21st at 8.15
SPECIAL RADIO GUEST NIGHT

"BIG HEARTED"
ARTHUR ASKEY
The Man who put the "WAQ" in BAND "WAQ"GON

SUPPORTED IN A
SPECIAL PROGRAMME

BY
CLARKSON ROSE'S

"TWINKLE" COMPANY

SUNDAY NEXT, ug. 28th at 8.15 p.m.
CLAPHAM AND DWYER

It's Better to Book in Advance and Costs no more !

COUNTY BOROUGH OF HASTINGS
WHITE ROCK PAVILION
Director of Entertainments: John Burton   Tel.: 1840

Commencing MON., JUNE 13th, for a SIX weeks season
MONDAY to FRIDAY at 7-45   SATURDAYS at 6-0 and 8-30
MATINEES: WEDNESDAYS at 3-0
Admission: 6/-, 5/-, 4/-, 3/-, 2/-. All Bookable
Box Office open daily 10—7-30; Sundays 11—12-30 & 3—5

COMPLETE CHANGE OF SHOW, SCENES AND DRESSES EACH WEEK

OLIVE FOX   CLARKSON ROSE

TWINKLE
THE CROWNING ACHIEVEMENT IN MUSICALS

17
IN THE GOOD OLD SUMMERTIME

Shows with holidaymakers much in mind packed the theatres and pier pavilions of the Sussex resorts from the late nineteenth century but it was from after the First World War, and generally until the mid-1960s, that the more spectacular and exciting productions were seen. Their guest artists were well known, usually because they had appeared in films or had been heard on radio. In later years many of them had already achieved some fame on television which, after the coronation of Queen Elizabeth, had become a more common feature in British households.

Among the regular summer visitors – in fact most of them were also residents of the county in whose resorts they appeared – were Sandy Powell (he and his wife, Kay White, had an hotel in Seaside, Eastbourne) with *Star Wagon*, Clarkson Rose with *Twinkle* (he lived in Meads, Eastbourne) and the *Fol de Rols* (the show's producer, Greatrex Newman, lived in Polegate). Another popular entertainer was Cyril Fletcher who for many years fronted a series of shows with his wife, Betty Astell. They lived at Buxted.

The *Fol de Rols* was billed as the show 'any child can take its parents to' . . . 'the show for high brows, low brows and no brows'. Despite this disclaimer, it was a show packed with novel ideas, witty lyrics and sharp sketches, much of it written by Greatrex Newman, whose drive and grasp of what was required in high class seaside resorts, firmly established their reputation nationally. *Fols* material was brighter, cleverer, more incisive than seaside audiences had been accustomed to and they lapped it up. For sixty years the tradition was maintained and

The Fols de Rols of 1920, at Scarborough with their founder, George Royle, sitting in the front with cane and cape.

if the *Fol de Rols* seat prices were higher than those of other seaside shows, this was because their production numbers were more lavish and their artists the best in their kind of business.

Clarkson Rose and his wife and co-star, Olive Fox, made a significant contribution to seaside entertainment. *Twinkle* was what might reasonably be called an 'end of the pier' show but there was never anything cheap and tawdry about it. 'Clarkie', as he was affectionately known, saw to it that over the forty years *Twinkle* entertained audiences along the Sussex coast its quality never diminished, its standards never declined. It was not always easy to gauge what audiences wanted, as he admitted in a letter to the *Eastbourne Gazette's* theatre critic in the 1960s:

'There are times when I have felt terribly frustrated, as a provider of shows, when I have included in my programme some really good sophisticated material, only to find that, with one or two exceptions, in the main audiences prefer stuff that doesn't challenge their perception too much. But this experience as a rule has generally been in the off-season. In the summer time, or at holiday time, the local audiences are augmented by an influx of visitors from all over the country, and their uptake and appreciation of first class material, in shows like the *Fol-de-Rols* and mine, is most refreshing.'

Unlike the other resorts, Brighton tended not to have summer shows and went in rather for different weekly bills. This policy was, however, becoming increasingly difficult to carry out and in 1959 the *Fol de Rols* played a season at the Theatre Royal. In the 1960s, *Take a Tripp,* featuring the long-established Sussex seaside favourite and former *Fols* star Jack Tripp, was presented on the Palace Pier. There were attempts in succeeding years to revive variety on the pier with stars such as Dick Emery, Elsie and Doris Waters, Ronnie Corbett and again, Jack Tripp. But from the 1960s summer shows failed to attract Brighton audiences.

Jack Tripp.

After the war Eastbourne enjoyed a remarkable variety of good summer shows. In the 1950s Avril Angers appeared at the Devonshire Park Theatre and Terry Scott at the Hippodrome. Denny Willis headed the bill at the Hippodrome and in 1956 the northern comic Norman Evans brought his show, *Over the Garden Wall,* there for a twelve week season.

In 1959 the *Fol de Rols* played a thirteen week season, including in their ranks Leslie Crowther, a young comedian who had begun his career as a Shakespearean actor at the Regent's Park Open Air theatre. In other years *Fols* bill toppers included Denny Willis, Don Arrol, Semprini, Bill Pertwee and Jack Tripp.

In 1958 Bruce Forsyth made *Gaytime* 'one of the most successful shows at the Hippodrome for years'. From here he went on to compere *Sunday Night at the London Palladium* and was succeeded in *Gaytime* by Ted Rogers, 'the new style comedian', who had already been in the pantomime at the Connaught in Worthing and had understudied Tommy Steele in panto at the Coliseum.

In the 1960s Eastbourne welcomed the elegant cleverness of TV's master magician David Nixon in *Showtime* to the Winter Garden and

Cyril Fletcher's *Masquerade* company to the *Hippodrome*.

For thirteen successive years, from 1946 until 1959, Cecil Johnson presented *Fun in the Air* at either the Redoubt or the Winter Garden. At

the Redoubt the bandstand was altered to make it an enclosure with dressing room facilities. Here, in the open air, always dependent on weather conditions, seven men and women, elegant

Fun in the Air at the Redoubt bandstand.

in full evening dress, battled for audiences.

The fact that 1,500 turned up for the opening night of the season of 1957 gives some idea of the show's popularity. But in the wet summer of 1958 there was, not surprisingly, a considerable drop in numbers.

When *Nights of Gladness* replaced Johnson's *Fun in the Air,* 1,100 paying customers turned up on the opening night and in later years Chips Sanders in *Redoubt Roundabout* received enthusiastic audiences whenever the weather was kind.

The shows at the pier theatre in Eastbourne regularly attracted good audiences. If Clarkson Rose was not there, Sandy Powell was. There were those who may at first have felt that a broad Yorkshire comedian would not go down too well in the 'Empress of Watering Places' but the show, *Star Wagon,* was an instant hit, as was its successor, *Starlight.* With the show's manager, Norman Meadow, as his straight man Sandy Powell, who was to receive the MBE in the 1975 Queen's Birthday Honours, filled the theatre night after night. Eventually they went on to form Southbourne Productions, which presented *Starlight* every summer until 1970. Each season there was a new production. The material was new, rarely rehashed stuff from the previous year. The cast usually included Bob Andrews, an experienced radio performer and story teller in dialects, as compere. Then there was Horace Mashford, also from radio and with a background in panto; singers Clive Stock and Gwen Overton who had appeared in *Brigadoon* and *Oklahoma*; Kay White, Sandy's wife, who was a pianist and character actress. She, along with the dancers, the eight Starlights, completed the cast. On occasions the Pier Dance Band with its popular singer, Susan Maughan, and led by Ronnie Hancox, joined the show and at a Sunday charity performance fronted by Sandy Powell (pictured right) and with the *Starlight* cast, the guest star was singer Frankie Vaughan.

Of the 1966 season the *Eastbourne Gazette* commented:

'None of the Sussex seaside towns is offering anything like the wealth of entertainment which Eastbourne is presenting for its many thousands of visitors this summer season. Brighton, four times as big as Eastbourne, is staging one summer show and a weekly helping of straight theatre. Hastings – one summer show and no straight theatre. Bexhill – one repertory company and no summer show. Worthing – one summer show. Compare Eastbourne's "enjoy yourself" recipe. The *Fol de Rols* at the Congress Theatre, *Starlight* at the Pier Theatre and the *Dazzle* show at the Royal Hippodrome. Three first class shows – each one presenting three programmes. At the Devonshire Park Theatre is a weekly production by the resident repertory company. At the Central Bandstand, Grand Parade, twice daily concerts by Britain's best military bands. And on Sundays there are some very excellent concerts at the Congress Theatre and the Pier Theatre.'

In 1945 the modest little Esplanade Theatre at Bognor, built on the site of an even more humble wooden bandstand where Tipper's Band had once been regular performers, underwent some important structural changes. It was given a roof and a somewhat flimsy proscenium arch of wood and canvas and underwent a name change too as if to emphasise its new importance. It was now the Esplanade Concert Hall. In 1951 the Esplanade Concert Hall was finally converted into a real theatre, its new name indicating the change that had taken place. At last the connection between successful holiday resorts and entertainment in comfortable surroundings had been made – and there was even central heating.

Bunny Baron's *Ripples of Mirth,* which had run for two seasons in 1946 and 1947; Hedley Claxton's *Gaytime;* and Eric Ross's *Dazzle* and *Flotsam Follies* brought to the Esplanade such quality acts as Elsie and Doris Waters; Clive Dunn (Corporal Jones in *Dad's Army*), Tony Hancock and Harry Worth. But Bognor's entertainment spots gave way before a variety of onslaughts, not least from the weather. In 1965 the seaward end of the pier vanished in a storm. Television was also demonstrating how it could confine thousands of former lovers of live entertainment to their armchairs. The pattern of theatre-going was being irrevocably altered.

Cyril Fletcher.

At Littlehampton at the end of the last century Professor Pelham's *Mirth, Magic and Mystery Show* had played at the converted St Saviour's Church for several seasons. He was succeeded by Harry Joseph's company which offered, in addition to summertime pierrot shows, winter programmes of pantomime and drama at both St Saviour's and the 500 seater Victoria Hall. Later, and until after the Second World War, there were several summer shows such as *Holiday Highlights* at the theatre called the Pavilion on the Green.

The White Rock Pavilion at Hastings had regular visits from the *Fol de Rols.* In the mid to late 1930s they were there starring, among others, the Western Brothers, Arthur Askey, Jack Warner and Cyril Fletcher. Cyril was back there after the war with his own *Masquerade* company and another summer show success at White Rock was *Out of the Blue* with casts which included the revue star Desmond Walter Ellis, Tommy Wallis, Don Smoothey and Tom Layton, and the popular TV comic duo, Terry Scott and Hugh Lloyd. The pier at St Leonards, never a resounding financial success, rarely succeeded in putting on top-line shows although there were some popular concert parties there in the early years such as Wilson James's *Gaieties*, Frank Dunlop's *Biscuits* and Edgar Allan Brown's three companies, which rotated in winter round the resorts with *Moonshine, Vogue* and *Charivari*.

After the war a number of successful shows were presented at Worthing's Pier Pavilion. There was *Show Box, Band Box, Box of Tricks* and then there was *Showtime*. Richard Jerome's *Gay Parade* featured Worthing resident, Bill Fraser, who before the war had been a significant figure in promoting the Connaught. Another show was *Evening Stars* which included Norman Vaughan.

There were many successful summer shows prior to the war at Bexhill's De La Warr Pavilion and notable among them was *All's Well*, a summer revue with a cast of twenty headed by Billy Merson, Dennis Noble and Zoe Wynn. Bertram Montague's *Bubbling Over* which lasted three seasons until 1949 was followed by *Gaiety Fair* starring Avril Angers. It was in 1951 that *Starlight Rendezvous* with comedian Freddie Frinton and Lucille Gaye came for the first time to Bexhill and played to record houses. In the course of the season the show was seen by 60,000 people and was similarly successful the following year. Bexhill audiences had fallen in love with Freddie and if they could not have him they did not want anyone else. When Sandy Powell replaced him for a season, audience numbers declined drastically which, considering Powell's enormous following at Eastbourne, was surprising. Freddie Frinton, by then a star at the London Palladium and about to team up on TV with Thora Hird in *Meet the Wife*, was persuaded to return for the 1957 and 1958 seasons and back came the audiences. A record 50,000 people saw the 1958 *Starlight Rendezvous* but the following year, when Billy Whittaker and Bill Pertwee topped the bill the numbers dropped right off again.

From 1961 Bexhill had no resident summer show. In the high season companies headed by a star name from television would fit a week at the De La Warr into their touring itinerary and the new names on the emerging pop scene – Cliff Richard and the Shadows, Marty Wilde, Matt Monro, Mark Wynter and Ricky Valance – would play one-night stands there. By the end of the 1960s it was the same all along the coast.

The summer shows were over.

18

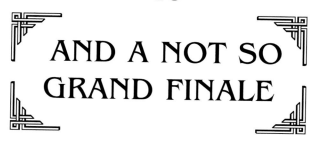

AND A NOT SO GRAND FINALE

Let us take a brief final peep round the curtain and pose a question or two. Where are the shows? Or rather, where have the audiences gone? What has happened to the huge crowds that turned out for Leno and Lloyd, lined the route Sarah Bernhardt took to the station to return to London after an afternoon performance in Brighton, queued for the *Fol de Rols,* bought last-night presents for the casts of their favourite summer shows? At Hastings they slept out in the streets, some of them, to see the arrival of the circus and year after year people came back to smaller resorts like Bognor and Littlehampton, often at their children's insistence, to see their favourite minstrels or pierrots.

So, where had the audiences gone? To the Costas every one? Relaxation of controls, improved communications and cheap air travel made holidays abroad available to all and at summer weekends there would be more people queuing for aeroplanes at Gatwick and Luton than at stations for trains or coaches to the seaside. And in the winter the all-the-year-round residents of the resorts no longer had to battle along wind-and-rain-lashed promenades to places of entertainment – they had it all at home, courtesy of the BBC and ITV, video and CD.

So at the beginning of the new millennium what is there in terms of live entertainment in our Sussex seaside resorts? How many venues remain? The Alhambras and Gaieties, Hippodromes and Regals and other theatres at Hastings and Brighton have all gone and the Esplanade at Bognor has disappeared with them. There are car parks or office blocks on the site of some of the theatres where Marie Lloyd sang, where the resident rep presented thrillers and farces and Max Miller winked at the boys and girls in the 'gods'. Was it because we thought that we did not need these places that led us to desert them? Is it just whimsy to think that they were essential to our lives?

But all is not lost. At Brighton the Theatre Royal still attracts fine plays with first-class casts. There is the Komedia, a theatre and cabaret bar with its witty productions and fascinating performers. The Dome and the Gardner Centre also offer opera, orchestral concerts, ballet, jazz in addition to one night stands by comedians, soloist musicians and lecturers. There is still some vibrancy here. And there is, of course, the Brighton Festival . . .

To take another example of imaginative planning – in 1999 the De La Warr had a Summer Fiesta Season, with dancers from Cuba, Africa and Brazil and the Sinfonia 21 Wind Ensemble in residence at the theatre introduced new and unfamiliar music. Its workshops and open rehearsals indicated a genuine wish to encourage the public actively.

It is precisely this positive approach to audiences that is in some areas so sadly lacking and which recently led the *Evening Argus* drama critic, referring to yet another dated thriller he had seen, to write: 'The time is ripe to ask whether such fare will ever attract a new and younger generation of theatregoers'.

It is undeniable that the needs of some of the young are catered for as far as music is concerned. In the summer of 1999 Eastbourne's Congress Theatre, the Connaught at Worthing, the De La Warr all had their share of pop concerts. But many of the surviving theatres along the coast seem unable to offer consistently attractive fare for their wider public. All of them have their successful productions but too frequently there is a thinness in what is on offer, a lack of fibre. This is not to suggest that theatres ought to be all Shakespeare, Shaw and Moliere but programmes ought not to be so incontestably lightweight that they are as forgettable as they are unappealing.

Only Eastbourne, at the time of writing, has a genuine show for the summer season. The Royal Hippodrome is offering *The Golden Years*, a celebration of 100 years of comedy, song and dance and this is heartening.

But the big summer shows like the *Fols* and *Twinkle* are no longer with us. Eastbourne's Redoubt Bandstand Theatre no longer exists. There is no *Dazzle* at Bognor, no *Starlight Rendezvous* at Bexhill.

Nevertheless it would be churlish to ignore some highlights of recent years. Along the coast there have been stage performances that stay long in the mind. Russian ballet groups, Rumanian opera, South American tango dancers have all brought their magic to seaside theatres. Touring companies have come with West End shows but it has to be admitted that the diet in some towns seems too often to consist of one-night stands with a pop group or some fading singing star.

If the piers are still there today they are differently used. They are still fine for sitting out in the daytime and on some of them you can still buy a pint of whelks and a beer or a cup of tea and a cake, but at night they change. The slot machines clatter in halls that once housed dance bands and nationally famed comedians while other elegant spaces perched over the sea are converted into night clubs and karaoke bars.

For the most part the outdoor entertainments have gone. Who these days would brave wind and rain to sit in a deckchair in front of a small stage, no matter if the quality of performance was high? All that reminds us of the past are the few buskers, present in most of the towns.

Occasionally there are pavement artists and some of these are astoundingly good. But there is an absence of acrobats and fire eaters, there are no wrestlers or barrel jugglers and the hurdy gurdy men have gone along with the `Ethiopian serenaders'.

So is the future for live entertainment at the Sussex seaside bleak? It is certainly still provided, although in penny packages, for theatres are costly to run and actors, singers, comedians put pressure on the civic purse. This is the dilemma that faces the providers. We can only hope that it can be resolved so that the variety of good quality entertainment at one time available to residents and holidaymakers along the coast can be assured for the future.

BIBLIOGRAPHY

A Brief History of Seaford by Marie Lewis. East Sussex County Library Services 1982
A Funny Way to Make a Living by Bill Pertwee. Sunburst Books 1996
A History of Eastbourne Pier by Bernard Polley. Unpublished ms 1997
Bexhill on Sea by Julian Porter. Tempus 1998
Brighton by Eric Underwood. Batsford 1978
Brighton: A Pictorial History by D Robert Elleray. Phillimore 1987
Brighton and Hove in old photographs by Judy Middleton. Alan Sutton 1998
Brighton: Old Ocean's Bauble by Edmund M Gilbert. Flame Books 1954
Brighton's Music Halls by David Adland. Baron Birch 1994
Can you hear me mother? by Sandy Powell. Jupiter Books 1975
Eastbourne Theatres and Summer Entertainments by Bernard Polley. Unpublished ms 1993
Fashionable Brighton by Antony Dale. Oriel 1967
Hastings and St Leonards by Gavin Haines. Alan Sutton 1997
Hastings: A Living History by David Thornton. Hastings Publishing 1987
Hastings in Old Photos by Pamela Haines. Alan Sutton 1991
Hove: A Pictorial History by Eddie Scott. Phillimore 1995
Kindly Leave the Stage by Roger Wilmut. Methuen 1985
Music Hall in Britain by D F Cheshire. David and Charles 1974
Promenades and Pierrots by Bill Pertwee. David and Charles 1979
Punch and Judy by Peter Fraser. Batsford 1970
Talent, Wonder and Delight by Anthony Adams and Robert Leach. Blackie 1976
The People's Palaces by Lynn Pearson. Barracuda 1991
The Playhouse on the Park by Edward Thomas. Friends of Devonshire Park Theatre 1997
The Story of Bexhill by L J Bartley. F J Parsons 1971

The Theatre Royal, Brighton by Antony Dale. Oriel 1980
Time to Spare in Victorian England by J Lowerson and J Myerscough. Harvester Press 1977
Victorian and Edwardian Brighton by John Betjeman and J S Gray. Batsford 1972
With a Twinkle in my Eye by Clarkson Rose. Museum Press 1951
Worthing Pier: A History by Dr Sally White. Worthing Museum 1996

Magazines
Call Boy
Sussex County Magazine

Newspapers
Bexhill Observer
Brighton Gazette
Eastbourne Herald
Evening Argus
Hastings Observer
Sussex Daily News
Sussex Express
West Sussex Gazette
Worthing Herald